EUROPEAN MANA

Recruitment

EUROPEAN MANAGEMENT GUIDES
General editor: Pete Burgess

Recruitment

Incomes Data Services

Institute of Personnel Management

© Institute of Personnel Management 1990

All rights reserved. No part of this publication may be reproduced, stored in a retrieval system, or transmitted in any form or by any means, electronic, mechanical, photocopying, recording or otherwise, without written permission of the Institute of Personnel Management, IPM House, Camp Road, Wimbledon, London SW19 4UX.

Phototypeset by Input Typesetting Ltd, London
and printed in Great Britain by
Short Run Press Ltd, Exeter, Devon

British Library Cataloguing in Publication Data
Recruitment.
  1. Personnel. Recruitment & selection. – (European management guides, 1).
  I. Incomes Data Services II. Institute of Personnel Management III. Series
  658.311

ISBN 0–85292–449–6

The views expressed in this book are the author's own, and may not necessarily reflect those of the IPM.

Contents

General introduction	x
Acknowledgements	xiii
Introduction: Recruitment in the European Community	xiv
European Community law	xv
International placement service	xvii

Chapter

1 Recruitment in Belgium   **1**
The labour market	2
Personnel planning	4
Informing the authorities	4
Work-force consultation	5
Using temporary workers	5
Finding the applicant	8
Agreed provisions	8
The official placement service	11
Recruitment agencies	12
Graduate recruitment	13
Using the press	15
Selection	16
Methods	16
Documents, etc.	17
Unsuccessful candidates	18
Appendix	19

2 Recruitment in Denmark   **21**
The labour market	21
Personnel planning	22
Official notification	22
Work-force consultation	22
'Atypical' work	23
Finding the applicant	24
The state placement system	25
New private agencies	26
Executive recruitment	26
Advertising media	27

	Application and selection	28
	Quotas and incentives	29
	Appendix	29
3	**Recruitment in France**	**31**
	The labour market	31
	Personnel planning	32
	Informing the authorities	32
	Work-force consultation	33
	Using part-timers and temps	33
	Finding the applicant	36
	Agreed provisions	36
	The state placement system	37
	Recruitment consultants	38
	Direct recruitment	40
	Graduate recruitment	42
	Application documents	44
	Selection	45
	Methods	45
	Privacy	46
	Employment incentives	47
	Young persons	47
	Women	48
	Disabled workers	48
	Long-term unemployed	49
	Military service	50
	Making the offer	50
	Handling rejection	50
	Work permits and papers	51
	Appendix	52
4	**Recruitment in Germany**	**54**
	The labour market	55
	Personnel planning	56
	Consulting the authorities	56
	Consulting the work force	56
	Using part-timers and temps	58
	Finding the applicant	62
	The Federal employment service	62
	Managers and specialists	64
	Recruitment consultants	67
	Recruiting graduates	70
	Using the press	73
	Application documents	75

Selection methods and procedures	77
Selection guidelines	77
Selection methods: rights and obligations	78
Anti-discrimination provisions	81
Employment incentives	82
Offer and acceptance	83
Role of the works council	83
The form of the offer	84
Work permits and papers	84
Appendix	86
5 Recruitment in Greece	**89**
The labour market	89
Personnel planning	91
Official notification	91
Using part-timers and temps	91
Finding the applicant	93
The state placement system	93
Finding professional and executive staff	94
Graduates	96
Advertising media	97
Selection	98
Offers and rejections	99
The form of the offer	99
Work permits	100
Appendix	100
6 Recruitment in the Irish Republic	**102**
The labour market	102
Personnel planning	104
Work-force consultation	104
Using part-timers and temps	104
Finding the applicant	105
The official placement system	105
Recruitment agencies and consultants	106
Advertising	107
Graduate recruitment	109
Application documents	109
Selection	110
Offer and rejection	112
Rejection of applicants	112
Work permits	112
Appendix	113

7 Recruitment in Italy	**114**
The labour market	114
Preparing for recruitment	115
Informing the authorities	115
Work-force consultation	116
Using part-timers and temps	116
Finding the applicant	117
The state placement system	117
Press advertising	121
Recruitment consultants	121
Executive search	122
Graduate recruitment	123
Application documents	124
Selection	124
Provisions in law	125
Employment incentives	125
Employment quotas	127
Making the offer	128
The form of the offer	128
Work permits and papers	128
Appendix	129
8 Recruitment in the Netherlands	**131**
The labour market	131
Personnel planning	133
Informing the authorities	134
Using part-timers and temps	134
Finding the applicant	135
Internal recruitment	136
External recruitment	136
State job placement service	137
Recruitment consultancies	138
Advertising in the media	140
Graduate recruitment	142
Selection	143
Making the offer	144
Handling rejected applicants	145
Grievances	145
Appendix	146
9 Recruitment in Portugal	**148**
The labour market	148
Personnel planning	149

	Consulting the authorities	149
	Consulting the work force	149
	Using part-timers and temps	150
	Finding the applicant	153
	The official placement system	153
	Private agencies	154
	Press advertising	154
	Managerial recruitment	155
	Recruiting graduates	156
	Application documents	156
	Selection	157
	Privacy provisions	157
	Anti-discrimination provisions	158
	Offer and acceptance	158
	The form of the offer	158
	Work permits	159
	Appendix	159
10	**Recruitment in Spain**	**161**
	The labour market	161
	Personnel planning	162
	Work-force consultation	162
	Official notification and recruitment procedures	163
	'Atypical' work	164
	Finding the applicant	166
	Agreed and statutory provisions	166
	Recruitment techniques	167
	Advertising in the media	167
	Employment agencies	168
	Graduate recruitment	168
	Application documents and selection	169
	Employment incentives	170
	Making the offer	171
	The contract of employment	171
	Job grading	172
	Work and residence permits	173
	Appendix	175
Further reading and information		**177**
	European organizations	177
	Selected reading and references	177

General introduction
European Management Guides

The growing involvement of British businesses in the European Community has imposed novel demands on managers. For many small and medium-sized companies the challenge has been to find new markets and consolidate service networks. Larger organizations have been swept up in a series of mergers, acquisitions, joint ventures, strategic reviews and rationalization. In both cases, managers with personnel responsibilities have seen their tasks expanded and redefined. Increasingly, this includes involvement, both direct and at arm's length, in the recruitment and management of employees in other member states of the European Community. In many organizations the human resource manager has become the key figure in integrating the individuals and cultures which make up an internationalized company.

Experience has shown, often painfully, that the management of people lies at the heart of whether an international joint venture, merger or acquisition succeeds or fails. And familiarity with the local culture and regulation of employment underpins any understanding of the opportunities and limitations facing key executives in a foreign subsidiary. Acquisitions in particular, with their inheritance of established employment law and industrial relations practices, can pose a special challenge to new management teams.

The European Commission's plans for new Community legislation on many aspects of employment, as a part of the 'social dimension' to the single European market, will bring national systems of employment law closer together. However, differences between cultures, institutions, law and practice will persist for the foreseeable future. Understanding and working with the grain of this diversity will be vital for any personnel or line manager entrusted with European responsibilities. Professional advice is indispensable in any European venture, but precious time and

General introduction

money can be saved by gathering information in advance before meeting lawyers, consultants or the local public authorities.

European Management Guides aim to meet this need for accessible and comprehensive information on employment in the countries of the European Community. The series, researched and written by Incomes Data Services Ltd, and published by the Institute of Personnel Management, consists of five handbooks covering:

- Recruitment.
- Terms and conditions of employment.
- Industrial relations.
- Pay and benefits.
- Training and development.

Each handbook will present information on a country-by-country basis, and will be structured to allow easy cross-country comparison. Extensive appendices detail local organizations which can provide further help and information. European Management Guides are not, however, intended as a substitute for expert advice, tailored to an individual situation and given as part of a professional relationship. Every effort has been made to ensure that the information contained in the handbooks is accurate and relevant. The publishers and authors offer them to readers on the understanding that neither organization seeks to take the place of either a lawyer or a consultant.

Incomes Data Services

Incomes Data Services has monitored employment developments in Europe since 1974. IDS's International Service publishes:

- *IDS European Report*, a monthly subscription journal on pay and employment law and practice in the European Community and Scandinavia. Each issue includes news on pay, collective bargaining and legal developments in Community countries, a Country Profile outlining recent developments, statistics and the economic background for individual countries, features, and regular statistics on pay, prices, labour costs and employment.
- *IDS International Documents*, two series of in-depth publications covering Commencement and Termination of Employment and Pay and Conditions on an individual country basis. Updated annually, each guide contains both context and detail for a single country in these central areas of human resource management.
- *1992: Personnel Management and the Single European Market*, published jointly with the Institute of Personnel Management.

For further details please contact: IDS Subscriptions, 193 St John Street, London EC1V 4LS (tel. 071-250-3434, fax 071-608-0949).

Acknowledgements

This handbook was researched and written by the International Department of Incomes Data Services Ltd, London. The series editor is Pete Burgess and contributions were also prepared by Angela Bowring, Andrea Broughton, Hanna Kazerani, Sally Marullo, Tony Morgan and Raili Seppanen. The authors are grateful to the many individuals and organizations, in the UK and in other EC member states, who provided information for the handbook and allowed themselves to be interviewed during the development of the series. We should specifically like to acknowledge the collaboration of Vincenzo Barrai (BSI Italia, Milan), Bill Robertshaw (Lisbon), John Piperoglou (Stedima Business Consultants, Athens), Bureau Berenschot (Netherlands) and Jorge Marques (APG, Lisbon). We also extend our gratitude to the panel of expert advisers drawn from the National Committees of the Institute of Personnel Management. Thanks are also due to the editorial staff of the IPM for their patient support.

Introduction
Recruitment in the European Community

Finding the right workers with the right skills in the right places has always been a central concern for organizations of all kinds. The task is likely to present new challenges in the 1990s, especially for companies whose business needs are driving them to look towards continental Europe. With the young and the qualified forecast to become scarcer and more expensive, finding and retaining people will play a crucial part in business success in the European Community.

This European Management Guide handbook on recruitment aims to meet the information needs of line managers and personnel professionals involved in overseeing or undertaking recruitment in the countries of the European Community. Each chapter deals with an individual country, with the recruitment process broken down into:

- An overview of recruitment conditions and the labour market.
- Statutory provisions on work-force consultation.
- Options other than full-time permanent recruitment.
- Finding the applicant: the role of the state employment service, employment agencies and headhunters, advertising media, and recruiting graduates.
- The law and practice of selection, offer and acceptance.
- An appendix listing organizations which can be turned to for help in tackling the local labour market, together with the prime media vehicles for job advertising.

The book begins with a short outline of how European Community law impinges on recruitment, and ends with a list of selected further reference material.

It does not set out to prescribe particular recruitment approaches or techniques. Some guidance both on the general issues raised by international recruitment as well as the specific questions which need to be asked when looking for an employment agency or a search consultant can be found in John Courtis's *Recruiting for Profit* and the study of executive search by the *Economist*, details of which are given in the suggestions for further reading at the end of the volume. Recruitment is an area in which do-it-yourself can be dangerous. In an unfamiliar labour market, decisions must be taken on the basis of local expertise. Whilst desirable throughout the recruitment process, such advice is imperative when turning to the conclusion of a local employment contract.

European Community law

European Community law currently makes few direct provisions on the recruitment process as such, although legislation together with rulings of the European Court of Justice have been central in shaping regulations and compensation in the area of sex discrimination. Planned directives, proposed by the European Commission as part of its Social Action Programme, will—if implemented—affect fields such as 'atypical' work, and the form of employment contract. We look at some of these issues in a little more detail below.

One central objective of the European Community is the facilitation of the free movement of goods, capital and labour. The free movement of workers and their families is enshrined in article 48 of the Treaty of Rome, and has been more precisely defined by a number of complementary directives and regulations. Spain and Portugal, which are still in transition to full membership of the Community, will not be fully subject to free movement until the beginning of 1993, the deadline for the implementation of the single European market. However, effective freedom of movement within the Community has been impeded by differences of language, the incongruence between national educational and training systems, incompatibilities between social security systems, rights of residence when not in employment, the incommensurability of vocational and professional qualifications, and lack of information about vacancies. A number of initiatives have been proposed in the context of the European Commission's Action Programme to implement the Social Charter, which address some of these outstanding problems.

The issue of comparability of qualifications is a central concern of recruiters, and the EC has initiated various measures to assist, some of which extend back to the mid-1960s. A number of specific directives regulate the mutual recognition of qualifications in particular sectors, such as health, the law, and architectural practice. The Directive on Mutual Recognition of Professional Qualifications (89/48), in force from January 1991, requires all member states to recognize higher educational diplomas awarded elsewhere in the Community, on completion of professional education and training lasting at least three years subject to the qualification being granted by a recognized body. Member states may require further demonstration of experience and a period of local adaptation under certain circumstances. A further directive covering vocational qualifications requiring less than three years' training has been submitted for discussion by the European Commission. CEDEFOP, the Community's training agency in Berlin, also publishes comparative lists of vocational qualifications which set out the equivalence of a broad range of attained manual and technical skills. Sectors covered so far include hotels and catering, motor vehicle repair, and construction. A future volume in this series of European Management Guides will look at systems of education and vocational training in the member states.

One area in which the impact of Community law has been very considerable is that of sex discrimination, equal pay and equal opportunities. The Treaty of Rome itself, two directives passed in the 1970s, and decisions of the European Court of Justice in Luxembourg have created a body of law which has been used by domestic courts throughout Europe to rule on cases of alleged sex discrimination. In line with EC directives, all member states have introduced regulations which proscribe discrimination in recruitment, and forbid any phrasing of a job advertisement which might suggest that either men or women would be more favoured. Enforcement, and the degree to which equal opportunities on grounds of sex or race are advocated positively, vary considerably between member states, however. Following an important ruling on sex discrimination on appointment, which was handed down by the European Court of Justice in 1984, compensation awards in sex discrimination cases can no longer merely restore out-of-pocket expenses incurred by a victim of discrimination but must also have a deterrent effect.

Terms and conditions for part-time workers have also been the subject of European Court deliberations on the issue of 'indirect discrimination'. In several rulings the Court has decided that because part-time work is overwhelmingly carried out by women, anything less than full *pro rata* treatment for part-timers in pay and agreed or statutory benefits could constitute a form of indirect sexual discrimination. Direct action to provide *pro rata* benefits for part-timers is proposed in a number of draft directives on so-called 'atypical' work produced by the European Commission in June 1990.

The three proposed directives on 'atypical work' aim to establish a standard EC-wide framework for the regulation of part-time work, fixed-term contracts, and employees of temporary work agencies. The main provisions, if accepted, would provide for equal access for part-timers and temporary workers to vocational training and company benefits, as well as a number of statutory benefits. Such employees would also be taken into account when calculating the size of the work force for determining the employment threshold at which employee representative bodies must be established. Employers would be required to consult workers' representatives about the use of atypical contracts, and in large firms produce a regular report on such employment. Temporary contracts lasting less than one year would not be allowed to be repeated such that the total period of employment exceeded three years. Temporary employees supplied by agencies would need to be informed of any major health and safety hazards, and this information, together with details of working hours, the skill levels required, and other features of the job to be filled would need to be set out in the assignment contract between the user employer and agency.

International placement service

Employers and work seekers have access to SEDOC, a pan-EC system for the notification of vacancies and placement. In the UK SEDOC is run by the Employment Service, which is part of the Department of Employment. The Overseas Placement Unit (OPU) is responsible for notifying local Job Centres of vacancies in other EC countries, and also uses the TV Oracle service. The OPU can also match speculative applications from work seekers against vacancies it receives through the system. UK vacancies can also be notified to official job placement systems in other member states, either because they are hard to fill or demand special skills, or because of a statutory requirement to give priority to EC citizens when a UK employer requests a work permit for an overseas worker. OPU also holds information, made available to applicants moving abroad, on living and working conditions in other Community countries. Although the system is computerized in the UK, it is not yet integrated at a European level, and the operation of SEDOC internationally is being reviewed to cope with the expected upturn of cross-border placement after 1992.

Appendix

The European Commission:
London office
Jean Monnet House
8 Storey's Gate
London SW1P 3AT
tel. 071–222 8122
fax 071–222 0900

SEDOC:
Employment Service
Steel City House
c/o Moorfoot
Sheffield S1 4PQ
tel. 0742–739190

CEDEFOP:
Bundesallee 22
1000 Berlin 15
tel. +49 30 884120

1
Recruitment in Belgium

Recruitment in Belgium by non-local organizations is complicated by the country's division along linguistic lines; in some circumstances political and religious differences also shape the cultural environment. Over half the Belgian population of nearly 10 million live in Flanders, in the north of the country, which is officially Flemish (Dutch)-speaking. Around a third live in the southern French-speaking provinces of Wallonia, whilst 10 per cent reside in the capital, Brussels, which is officially designated as bilingual. There are a small number of German-speakers in the east.

These divisions mean that, although Belgium is a small country, the labour market is still split to some extent between the French and Flemish-speaking communities. In the last decade this has been paralleled by devolution of many formerly national responsibilities to regional and community administrations. The Flemish are more likely to be bilingual (with French or English as a second language) or trilingual than the Walloons and thus have greater employment opportunities, although there is still great reluctance to cross the cultural divide in work.

The structure of organizations also reflects these divisions and therefore they usually function on a regional rather than national basis—either operating autonomously in both main regions or in just one. Similarly, the press either finds its readership exclusively in one region or publishes separate editions in French and Flemish.

Under national legislation, undertakings operating in Belgium must use the language of the region in which they are located for all legal instruments and documentation, including communications with their staff. The Flemish regional executive has defined this further, requiring all individual and collective contracts, both oral and written, to be in Flemish. Thus non-Belgian recruiters will need to familiarize themselves with the networks which operate in the region where they are set up. Most executive employment is in Brussels, and many organizations functioning in this area cater for French and Flemish and often also English-speakers.

Otherwise the most salient feature of the recruitment scene in Belgium is the existence of a national agreement on recruitment and selection procedures which, although mostly having only moral force, provides a framework and guidelines within which recruiters operate.

The labour market

Belgium's labour force totals some 4,120,000 people, out of a total population of almost 9,900,000. Although the labour force grew at 3 per cent during the 1980s, the overall activity rate plummeted from 46 per cent in 1977 to 36 per cent by 1988. This can be explained in a number of ways.

In common with other European countries, the birth rate has dropped dramatically over the last ten years and the population is increasingly an ageing one. At the same time, and partly as a response to the recession of the early 1980s, working life has been shortened by:

- Extending schooling, at least on a part-time basis, up to the age of 18.
- Early retirement—in a few industries as early as the age of 50.
- Introduction of career breaks.

The decade has also seen a marked reduction in activity rates for young men (14–25) and older men (50–64), accompanied by a rise in female participation, particularly in the 25–49 age group, from 47 per cent to 64 per cent.

Although only around 10 per cent of total employment is part-time—lower than in most other EC states—this represents a significant rise compared with the late 1970s. In 1988 there were 343,000 part-time jobs in the economy, a 59 per cent rise over the decade: 80 per cent of these were undertaken by women. And whilst only 2 per cent of men were employed part-time, this form of employment occupied 23 per cent of women. Part-time employment is particularly prevalent in business services (including banking and insurance), which saw a 30,000 growth in jobs over the period, and 'other services' (covering some public services like transport), where there was a 22,000 increase. Together these two sectors account for 80 per cent of the part-time jobs in the economy. Only 2·3 per cent of the working population (3·3 per cent of employees) are temporaries who are treated as the employees of temporary employment agencies which hire out their services.

Official estimates put employment in 1988 at approximately the same level as ten years earlier. However, whereas private-sector employment has fallen by some 7 per cent over the decade, public-sector jobs increased by 10 per cent. Translated onto a regional basis, employment in French-speaking Wallonia in the south, where heavy industry bore the brunt of the two oil shocks, dropped by 14 per cent, and the Brussels region saw an 8 per cent drop. In contrast, Flemish-speaking Flanders in the north witnessed a 4 per cent increase in jobs, which is making for a particularly tight labour market across a whole range of skills at present. Recruitment of labour from the French-speaking community is increasing, although such personnel are less likely to have the necessary language skills required.

The boom of the late 1980s, together with the forthcoming single European market, which has attracted operations to Belgium, may have stimulated a rise in private-sector employment. The official forecasting office, the Bureau du Plan, estimate a net annual increase of 39,000 jobs between 1990 and 1995. Companies appear to be experiencing greater difficulties in recruiting staff, suggesting persisting structural imbalances, given that unemployment in 1990 was running at just under 9 per cent—higher than the EC average.

Recruitment problems are likely to be exacerbated by the continuing fall forecast for the number of school leavers. By 1995 the total is projected to fall by 8 per cent from its 1987 level. This trend will be reflected in the changing age composition of the population, with the 0–14 age group set to fall from 20 per cent of the population in 1980 to 16·5 per cent by the year 2000, and the 60+ group to increase from 18·5 per cent to 22·6 per cent over the same period. In addition to the overall shortage of school leavers, there is also a problem of under-qualification, particularly so far as the supply of young people holding A2 and A3 technical subject school leaving certificates is concerned, paralleling increasing demand for administrative workers who are bi- or trilingual.

As part of the national framework agreement concluded for 1989/90, which affects the terms and conditions of 75 per cent of employees in the private sector, a sum equivalent to 0·18 per cent of each firm's wage bill has been allocated to a special training fund for 'at risk' groups in the labour market, which include unqualified school leavers. Females are more likely to lack qualifications than males, and special measures are being taken to encourage girls to take up technical options once basic schooling is completed. Similarly the Ministry of Labour is encouraging sectors and firms to take initiatives which will steer more women to train in jobs which have traditionally been seen as a male province.

Personnel planning

Informing the authorities

Under legislation passed in 1969, organizations which on average employ twenty or more staff must inform the official job placement service in their area (or the area where the vacancy has arisen) if the position has been vacant for three days, or is to be advertised in the press. This may be done by telephone. Employers must give details of the trade/profession (most manual and non-specialist white-collar jobs are classified according to an individual industry system), qualifications sought, remuneration and other main terms and conditions.

The placement service may then check:

- Whether the job falls within regulations governing public decency.
- Whether it is categorized as dangerous or involves handling dangerous substances (where prior medical examination is required).
- The location of the job (for example, whether it involves home work).
- The working time schedules (that is, whether it involves night work).
- Whether the pay offered conforms to minimum rates laid

down in the relevant sectoral collective agreement covering the enterprise. (Although most collective agreements are broadly along industry/sectoral lines—with most industries having separate agreements for blue- and white-collar staff—there is an agreement (*C.P. Nationale auxiliaire pour employés, No. 218*) which lays down minimum rates for all white-collar workers not specifically covered by any industry agreement).

Work-force consultation

Works councils (*conseils d'entreprise*) were created by statute in 1948 and must be set up in every private establishment employing at least 100 workers. They are joint bodies and comprise between six and twenty-two workers' representatives, according to the undertaking's size. Their functions are advisory and they have a right to information on the firm's employment structure, levels and forecasts. They must also be kept informed of any proposals to use part-time or temporary staff, since in some circumstances their approval must be obtained before staff are hired.

Following Belgium's recent history of collective redundancies following the two oil shocks, works councils are also entitled to examine the firm's criteria for recruiting and dismissing staff. Sectoral agreements may give works councils further functions in the area of use of temporary workers, job creation (particularly amongst at-risk groups) and induction procedures.

Using temporary workers

The practice of using temporary workers developed during the 1950s but the sector was not regulated until 1976. Temporary legislation passed that year established that the employment contract was between the temporary workers and the employment agency, with a contract for services between the client organization and the agency. At the time, this arrangement was opposed by the largest trade union confederation, the socialist-orientated Fédération Générale des Travailleurs de Belgique (FGTB), which wanted client organizations to be treated as the employers. It supported a state monopoly on placement. This legislation ran out in 1981 when a national collective agreement on temporary working (*Convention collective de travail No. 36 du 27.11.81 portant des mesures conservatoires sur le travail temporaire, le travail intérimaire et la mise de travailleurs à la disposition d'utilisateurs*) was negotiated on the tripartite National Labour Council (CNT) which, together with later amendments, defines temporary work, regulates the temporary work contract and lays down provision on the supplying of workers to client companies.

Temporary workers may be used only in four circumstances:

- As a stand-in when a permanent employee's contract has been temporarily suspended—for example, for health reasons.
- As a temporary replacement for a permanent worker whose contract has been terminated by notice. The duration of such an assignment is limited to three months and may be extended once, provided trade unions in the undertaking agree. If a worker has been dismissed for gross misconduct, such an assignment may last six months with trade union approval.
- Owing to an exceptional increase in work load, subject to the trade unions' approval of bringing in a temporary. Employers have to give unions details of the number of workers involved and the period concerned. In these circumstances temporaries would be engaged on monthly contracts, which may be renewed.
- To perform work of an exceptional and occasional nature—categories of which are defined by law—which would include, for example, stocktaking.

In practice the most frequent recourse to an agency is made in the second instance (i.e. a temporary replacement), since no union consultation is initially required for a three-month assignment. Manual workers are frequently taken on as temporaries to fulfil unforeseen orders; other options management might consider in such circumstances would include increasing overtime within permitted legal limits or the reorganization of working time into annualized hours.

Temporaries are permitted in all kinds of activity, including the public sector, but are banned in construction, furniture storage and removal services.

The contract between the temporary and the agency, and the one between the agency and the client company, must both be in writing. If a temporary does not sign a contract of limited duration within two days of starting an assignment, then the arrangement will be construed as a open-ended contract with the agency. A client company is responsible for ensuring that all employment regulations apply to temporaries, and their pay must be at the same rate as that of permanent workers doing the same job even though the agency makes payment. Temporaries are also included in the work-force for the purpose of determining the size of employee representative bodies. Legislation in 1987 confirmed the constitution of a joint committee for the temporary sector (such as exists for most other sectors) which would set basic terms and conditions. All its members have yet to be nominated.

Temporary agencies must be accredited annually by the employment authorities in the regions in which they operate. Rules are set separately by each of Belgium's constituent regions and cover the agency's aim, its capital and its obligations to its employees. In practice, large temporary agencies are accredited in all three regions. The 1981 agreement and subsequent legislation of 1987 require agencies (like employers elsewhere in the private sector) to contribute to social funds for temporaries to provide extra payments in the event of collective redundancy, or sickness.

There are currently more than seventy accredited temporary employment businesses in Belgium, some specializing in particular types of staff, such as nurses, computing staff, executives, and senior secretaries. Over half (with a 90 per cent share of the market between them) are members of UPEDI (Union Professionnelle des Entreprises de Travail Intérimaire) which in turn is a member of CIETT, the international trade association. UPEDI has a Code of Ethics which ensures quality of service to clients and also protects temporaries. The reputation of temporary agencies has increased over recent years. A pre-selection test is normally required of potential temporaries and a post-assignment debriefing is usual. Often temporary agencies are requested by clients to provide pre-selection tests for permanent posts as part of the trend for in-house personnel departments to farm out parts of their function.

T-Service Interim, established by statute in 1978, is the autonomous state temporary employment agency, with some 250 branches. It competes directly with private-sector organizations. Its charges are governed by statute and its board is jointly managed (employer/trade union). It has an average 30 per cent of the market nationally, ranging from 20 per cent to 40 per cent by region.

Some 70 per cent of temporaries are under 30 years of age and only 9 per cent over 40: 62 per cent are men. Overall 60 per cent are blue-collar workers (83 per cent in the case of male temporaries, compared with 42 per cent of women). Forty per cent of jobs done on a temporary basis for a period of over three months result in a permanent job offer being made. Temporary agencies are increasingly being used by job seekers to find permanent positions and by client companies to pre-select candidates. The most recent economic upturn has meant that many jobs which were initially filled on a temporary basis became permanent.

Finding the applicant

Agreed provisions

There is a national collective agreement (No. 38) on the recruitment and selection of workers, the *Convention collective de travail No. 38 concernant le recrutement et la śelection de travailleurs*, which was concluded by the main employers' and trade union organizations represented on the tripartite National Labour Council in 1983. It is morally binding in its entirety and covers a number of important areas. However, certain clauses which relate to obligations on employers have also been made legally binding through a royal decree dated 11 July 1984. The agreement sets out provisions on all aspects of recruitment, and we refer to it at the appropriate steps in the process.

Information to be given to the applicant. Under collective agreement No. 38, the employer must give the following information to candidates:

- A description of job duties.
- The job requirements, including training, experience, responsibilities.
- The location of the job, unless it cannot be defined in advance.
- The job application procedure.
- Whether the recruitment exercise is being conducted in order to build up a recruitment reserve.

Equal treatment. Under the terms of the collective agreement, employers must not treat candidates in a discriminatory manner. During recruitment and selection employers must make no distinction based on personal factors with no bearing on the job or the nature of the company, unless the law permits or requires it, as with the partial ban on night work for women and for all young people. There is in fact very little case law which relates to discrimination during the recruitment and selection process.

The Belgian constitution embodies the principle of equality of treatment, which outlaws discrimination of a direct or indirect nature, and applies specifically to access to employment, recruitment and selection procedures, placing an obligation on employers, those recruiting on behalf of employers and those responsible for processing and placing job advertisements. Sex may be a qualification for employment only in certain categories, defined by royal decree, such as in the performing arts, in certain personal care services or where night work is involved. Both the Flemish and the French communities have additional decrees relating to equal treatment. Sex equality legislation does not preclude positive action for women in jobs where they are under-represented, and advice on this issue may be obtained from the Ministry of Labour, Women's Section.

Legislation approved in 1981 outlaws racism in such areas as the provision of goods and services. There is a theoretical requirement for firms employing over twenty people to engage a certain number of disabled people. However, as yet there has been no decree implementing this legislation.

Respect for privacy. National agreement No. 38 also specifies that an applicant's private life must be respected during recruitment and selection. Questions about it are justified only if they relate to the job or to the conditions under which it is to be performed. Thus questions about marriage plans, or starting a family, would be unacceptable. This places an obligation not only upon the employer but also on other persons who are involved in recruitment and selection.

There is in fact very little law which relates to privacy, hence there is no absolute ban on questions (for example) about health, but care needs to be taken that such questions are handled in a non-discriminatory way. Freedom of contract is an underlying principle of the legal system and therefore there are few restrictions on the kinds of enquiries employers can make during the period when a decision is being reached. Verification of qualifications and previous employment history is fairly standard practice, however. Although investigations into financial standing and life style are not proscribed by law they are seldom conducted. Employees have a right (in some cases theoretical, since they are seeking a job) to withhold information or even give false information. Case law suggests that there is unlikely to be any remedy for the prospective employer in the latter case if the information concerned does not relate directly to the job.

Confidentiality. Employers must treat all information on candidates confidentially, according to the agreement. Likewise, applicants are required to participate in the selection process in good faith and furnish all necessary information on education, professional qualifications and previous employment experience relevant to the vacant post. Applicants must on their part refrain from divulging confidential information on the company which has been obtained during the selection procedure.

Other points of the national agreement require that the selection procedure must be conducted within a reasonable period of time. If it involves practical tests, the process may not last longer than is necessary to conduct them. There is case law in the area of payment for practical tests conducted within a selection procedure and whether this can be construed as proof of the existence of an employment relationship.

Sectoral collective agreements. The terms and conditions of around 75 per cent of employees in the private sector are affected by industry or sectoral-level collective agreements. Some of these are binding only on firms affiliated to the employers' organizations which are signatories to the agreement, but most have been extended by statute to cover all firms in a particular industry or sector. Agreements of this type, which are negotiated by joint industry committees (*commissions paritaires*), set minimum wage rates and other basic terms and conditions. Many industries also have job classification systems for blue- and white-collar employees into which advertised job vacancies will fit. In addition, some industry or sectoral agreements may have special provisions on recruitment.

The official placement service

There are few restrictions on which organizations may deal with job placements. However, the official placement service, which has now become a regional responsibility, and is thus dealt with by three organizations, retains a monopoly of placement in the public services. Otherwise companies are free to use the official service, the myriad private agencies or to advertise directly, as they please. Resort to external recruitment to fill vacancies is very much the norm, though tighter labour markets in recent years have caused firms to put more resources into their in-house training programmes.

As a result of recent constitutional changes, the latest of which were approved in 1988, the National Employment Office (Office National de l'Emploi, Rijksdienst voor Arbeidsvoorziening) has been restructured and now deals only with matters relating to unemployment and the payment of benefits. Job placement has therefore been completely devolved to the regional and community authorities. Use of official placement services is more common at the lower skill end of the market, reflecting the fact that none of the regional placement agencies has a specialist section dealing with executive recruitment. Opinions on the efficiency of the official services vary, depending on the type of staff sought and the region where the company is located. There seems to be less dissatisfaction with the service in Flanders, which has been established longer, but still it is regarded as bureaucratic. The official service is a relative newcomer to the field of placement and is competing with private agencies, many of which have been operating over several decades and therefore have built up well qualified and experienced work forces. However, the official service does have a cost advantage over private agencies.

FOREM (Formation-Emploi, the Office Communautaire et Régional de la Formation Professionnelle et de l'Emploi) is the *regional* (that is, for Wallonia in the south of the country) and *community* authority (for French-speakers in Wallonia and in the capital, Brussels, and for German-speakers in the eastern provinces) responsible for placement and training. It is administered by a joint management committee with responsibility for the day-to-day running of the service. The aims of the service are defined by the Regional Executive Council of Wallonia. The service is still in the process of establishing itself, following the 1988 reforms.

VDAB (Vlaamse Dienst voor Arbeidsbemiddeling en Beroepsopleidung) exercises the same functions for the Flemish-speaking area in the north of Belgium and for Flemish-speakers in the capital. The employment and vocational training services in Flanders were established in 1984 but functions were further defined in 1988. VDAB consists of a headquarters and a network of seventy-nine local placement offices. Employers are charged a nominal fee by law—which is often not enforced. An average of 7,500 jobs are handled monthly and there is a computerized vacancy notification system. Placements through VDAB account for 45 per cent of manual jobs filled in the region but only 7 per cent of managerial posts. There is a separate network of nine psychological centres where, for a fee, employers can arrange for candidates to be tested and job applicants may seek free advice. Use of the official placement service is not a condition for either group who wish to avail themselves of the centres' services. These centres also run pre-selection services.

ORBEM (Office Régional Bruxellois de l'Emploi) undertakes job placement for *all* workers in the Brussels region.

Recruitment agencies

Larger companies are more inclined to be directly involved in recruitment and selection, though even they are increasingly contracting parts of these procedures to agencies and consultancies. The many small firms in Belgium make extensive use of recruitment agencies. Private employment agencies are well established and numerous in all parts of the country and very little restriction is placed on their activities. They are principally used to find both white-collar and executive staff—less often manual employees. At the more qualified end of the market there are recruitment agencies specializing in graduates and in recruitment by function, such as for sales and marketing, PR, secretarial, computing, banking, finance and accountancy, and health service staff. Charges vary from Bf 20,000–40,000 (£325–£700), depending on the length and complexity of the search and the extent to which it involves advertising.

There are over 110 firms (or subsidiaries of parent companies) specializing in executive search and selection, the vast majority of which are based in Brussels, where over half the country's executive employment is to be found. Agencies may either draft and place press advertisements and/or pre-select candidates, often using psychological and graphological tests, or carry out purely search functions when recruiting senior managers. A full search service at the top end of the range would normally entail a fee of 30 per cent of annual salary.

Ascobel is an association representing professionals engaged in all kinds of consulting activities, including human resources.

Graduate recruitment

Belgium has a traditional education structure, and the formal qualifications demanded by employers closely match those gained at higher education institutions. Employment after graduation is very much dictated by the choice of degree subject. However, there is a feeling that education is too theoretical and does not properly equip the newly qualified for the world of work. Many companies therefore offer quite extensive periods of training to bridge this gap. Similarly, the official training agencies run work experience programmes, including programmes for graduates, and this is often a route to a permanent job offer. Technological change means that employers are seeking employees with a high degree of adaptability, which is not obvious from formal qualifications and may explain the prevalence of psychological and other tests. Employers are also looking for mobile qualified recruits with language skills, whilst recent surveys indicate the average job seeker looks for stability and security in employment.

University-level education is available at seventeen universities and other institutions of higher education, both state and private, though both enjoy substantial public subsidy. These tend to operate fairly autonomously but with some co-ordination between institutions in the same region. Six of these have university status: Universitaire de l'Etat at Liège, Rijksuniversiteit te Gent, Universitaire Catholique de Louvain, Katholieke Universiteit te Leuven, Universitaire Libre de Bruxelles and Vrije Universiteit de Brussel. Each university has a varied reputation according to subject area. Other higher education institutes do not provide the full range of university courses but specialize in certain subjects or courses within the individual stages. For example, the

Universitaire Instelling Antwerpen offers only second and third-stage courses.

A number of higher education institutions offers MBAs, since there are no business schools, which are regarded by some employers as icing on the cake. However, this qualification is not particularly sought after and is more the product of recessionary times, when even the higher qualified were in plentiful supply. It has also provided a route by which graduates with no business specialism can change tack.

An increasingly popular way of contacting graduates, particularly given the prevailing shortages of newly qualified people with a technical specialism, is through graduate fairs, which each university or institution of higher education runs annually during the academic year; they normally last between one and three days. Events may be organized by the institutions themselves, by student organizations or by private companies. Companies are invited to make formal presentations at these events and then have the opportunity to mingle with recent or aspiring graduates on an informal basis. It is on such occasions that direct approaches may be made by employers to students. It is not customary for graduates to fix themselves up with jobs far in advance of qualifying. In the case of men, some have still to discharge military service obligations before they are free to enter the job market.

There is no national system of university careers advice and job placement. A few universities directly run advisory and placement services, though quite often the latter are run in conjunction with organizations representing former students; in a few instances they are run by individual faculties. Some such services issue regular vacancy bulletins, circulated to former and current graduates. Advisory services may also give guidance on making unsolicited job applications. Contact with particular faculties or even individual professors is an additional means of access to graduates seeking employment. Lists of job seekers generated in this way may be made available to outside bodies.

Since the situation is so diverse, employers need to familiarize themselves with the facilities offered by each higher education institution.

Every Tuesday during the summer months the Flemish daily *De Standaard* runs a job column ('Pas Afgestudeerd') devoted to graduate job seekers. Similarly *Het Laatste Nieuws*, and *Le*

Soir for francophone Belgium, have Tuesday supplements entitled 'Jong Talent' and 'Mon Premier Emploi' respectively. *Intermédiaire*, a weekly appearing in French and Flemish specializing in job advertisements (though not just aimed at graduates), does carry articles on graduate recruitment and specific areas of the job market. A directory entitled *Move Up*, again available in both official languages, gives information on companies recruiting during the year, including types of vacancies, formal and personal qualifications sought and tests performed. Two student magazines, *Univers Cité* and *Campus*, respectively for French and Flemish students also carry job advertisements.

Using the press

The press is extensively used directly by employers and by recruitment agencies and consultants for advertising jobs at all levels. Public authorities have to advertise vacancies in the press, and if they are for organizations on a national level, then both the Flemish and the French press have to be used.

The rules on job advertisements are not particularly rigid. Advertisements must comply with the spirit of race discrimination and sex equality legislation, and certain aspects of employment law. Thus advertisements must not specify an applicant's sex (except in categories defined by royal decree—see above) and must make it clear that jobs are open to both sexes.

Pay rates are rarely mentioned in advertisements except by some Anglo-Saxon companies. Collectively agreed minimum pay scales by which most employers are bound (though most pay in excess of these) are based on skill level for manual workers, and usually on age or seniority for white-collar staff. Thus older but not necessarily more experienced staff tend to be paid at higher rates. (Managers fall outside the scope of such pay agreements, and their pay is therefore based entirely on market rates.) This underscores the importance of hierarchy in employment, and employers will often advertise for recruits in a particular age group so that they 'fit in' with the age profile of the existing work force. In addition, it is common for an advertisement to give details about the company and its business.

Press advertisements normally invite applications initially by telephone or by submission of a *curriculum vitae*, often specifying a handwritten supporting letter of application. Companies may not use fictitious job advertisements to publicize their own activities.

There is no national newspaper in Belgium, owing to the linguistic divisions in the country. The largest-circulation 'quality' daily newspaper in Flemish is *De Standaard*. It carries job advertisements every day, covering a wide variety of positions, and an executive supplement (*Personeelsgids*) in its weekend issue. The paper has a policy of carrying jobs advertisements only in Dutch or English. *Le Soir* serves a similar function for francophone Belgium, with over 2,000 jobs appearing weekly, over half of which are middle and senior management positions, many of them featuring in the weekend edition. It publishes advertisements in all languages. The *Gazet van Antwerpen* and *La Libre Belgique* are other important newspapers.

The local press, including free newspapers, also carries advertisements for a diversity of jobs, including those at executive level.

The Roularta media group through its *Carriere* division organizes job columns in a number of its own publications in both French and Flemish, including *Knack*, *Trends*, *Le Vif/l'Express*, *Trends/Tendances* and *Industrie*. There are also some specialist publications such as *La Semaine Informatique* (for computing posts), *Ingenieursblad/Journal des Ingénieurs*. Geres run a monthly bulletin to which readers can take out an annual subscription, giving details of job seekers in specified categories.

Selection

Methods

There are few limitations on the methods of selection which may be used by employers. Most applications, except for blue-collar jobs, would in the first instance be made through submitting a *curriculum vitae*, with a supporting letter of application (often handwritten). Job seekers are often warned about the importance of using correct forms of address and/or salutation. Photos are rarely requested.

Graphology tests are widespread, both as a pre-selection procedure or to back up impressions of candidates gained through other parts of the selection procedure. Psychological tests are also well known, though there is a tendency to use them more for older candidates or those who have applied for posts of considerable trust. Intelligence and aptitude tests are also standard. Other methods such as astrology or bio-rhythm testing are rare. Screening procedures are usually carried out by third parties (partly owing to the specialized skills involved in administering them) even in the case of large organizations. Once the short list is arrived at, much store is set by the interview, the conduct of which is governed by a number of issues covered by the national collective agreement dealt with above.

Employers do not have to reveal details of all the tests they intend to use in selection, but recruitment culture in Belgium is quite open and therefore most employers would give such information. They would also normally obtain a potential recruit's consent if graphology or other tests were to be employed.

Under collective agreement No. 38 any costs of tests or examinations organized as part of the selection procedure must be borne by the employers, if they have requested them, even if they are actually conducted by a third party.

Documents, etc.

References. It is customary to take up personal references, and it is often done by telephone. Employers do not usually seek evidence of a clean police record, since such vetting is a lengthy and bureaucratic procedure except in highly sensitive posts.

Return of documents. The national agreement stipulates that, if an applicant is not short-listed, the employer must return any documents that accompanied the job application within a reasonable period of time, so that they may be used to support other applications.

Submission of stamped and certified copies of documents. The employer may request stamped and authenticated supporting documents (such as diplomas, certificates or attestations) only *after* the selection has been made, according to the agreement. Since the preparation of such documents can involve the candidates in expense, their submission is limited to occasions where a job offer is certain. (Such documents are much more likely to be required in Belgium than would be the case in the United Kingdom.)

Successful applicants would expect to receive confirmation of the job offer in writing, with details of grade, pay, hours and the location of the workplace.

Work permits. There is equality of employment rights between workers of Belgian nationality and citizens of other EC member-states. (This does not apply to *all* holders of British passports, which do not automatically give entitlement to free circulation within the EC.) No work permits or any other special procedures are required for EC nationals. Citizens of other European countries, including at present Greece and Spain, together with Tunisia and Morocco, or their employer can apply for a Type A permit which is indefinite and for all occupations: the main condition is prior residence and employment. A Type B permit is restricted to one activity and employer, and is valid for up to two years: it is only issued when no suitable EC nationals are available.

Medical examination. It is obligatory for some types and categories of employee to undergo a medical as a condition of employment; they must also be regularly examined once recruited. This includes employees under 21, jobs where there is a risk of occupational disease, or jobs which involve using vehicles, cranes or potentially dangerous machinery. Otherwise, job offers may be made conditional upon the satisfactory outcome of a medical examination, at the employer's discretion.

Unsuccessful candidates

Certificate of attendance. If unemployed applicants have to report to the local unemployment office to qualify for benefit, they are entitled under the national agreement to ask a prospective employer for a certificate of attendance at a job selection exercise. This would confirm the time and date of attendance and, in relevant cases, the reasons why they were not selected for the job. (Until recently most unemployed people drawing benefit were subject to daily reporting; this has recently been changed to twice-monthly registration.)

Informing unsuccessful applicants. Applicants who meet the requirements of a post but are not selected must be informed of the employer's decision within a reasonable period. The national agreement specifies that if a candidate is more highly qualified than is specified by the employer it does not constitute a valid reason for rejecting the application.

Appendix

Organizations

National Employment Office:
boulevard de l'Empereur 7
1000 Brussels
tel. +32 2 510 20 11 (French-speakers)
+32 2 513 89 42 (Flemish-speakers)

FOREM:
boulevard de l'Empereur 5
1000 Brussels
tel. +32 2 510 20 11

VDAB:
Kaiserslaan 11
1000 Brussels
tel. +32 2 506 1599

ORBEM:
boulevard Ansprach 65
1000 Brussels
tel. +32 2 513 78 20

Ministry of Labour:
rue Belliard 53
1040 Brussels
tel. +32 2 230 90 10

Sécrétariat de la Commission du Travail des femmes
(information on positive action for women):
rue Belliard 51
1040 Brussels
tel. +32 2 233 40 16

Collective Industrial Relations Service (for copies of industry/sectoral collective agreements):
rue Belliard 51
1040 Brussels
tel. +32 2 233 41 49

Conseil National du Travail (for copies of national collective agreements):
avenue de la Joyeuse Entrée 17–21
1040 Brussels
tel. +32 2 233 88 11

Fédération des Enterprises de Belgique (largest employers' organization):
rue Ravenstein 4
1000 Brussels
tel. +32 2 515 08 11

Ascobel (Association Belge des Conseils en Organisation et Gestion):
avenue Louise 430/12
1050 Brussels
tel. +32 2 648 10 55
fax +32 2 646 05 41

Publications

Le Soir:
rue Royale 112
1000 Brussels
tel. +32 2 217 77 50
fax +32 2 217 07 84

De Standaard:
avenue Gossetlaan 30
1720 Brussels
tel. +32 2 467 27 00
fax +32 2 444 30 93

Carriere:
boulevard Emile Jacqmain 95
1000 Brussels
tel. +32 2 211 08 11
fax +32 2 218 05 32

Move Up directory:
Leonard & Partners
boulevard August Reyes 55–8
tel. +32 2 734 93 02

2
Recruitment in Denmark

New legislation, in force from summer 1990, has changed the context of job placement, creating new opportunities for both profit-making and non-profit-making organizations to develop employment services, especially in areas where particularly rigorous selection and research are called for. The trade unions have also traditionally played a role in placement across the spectrum of occupations, and this is likely to develop in the future. Regulation in the area of recruitment is comparatively low, but the climate of industrial co-operation encourages employee involvement in the elaboration of workplace personnel policies.

Local issues include:

- A high turnover rate.
- Low geographical mobility on the part of employees, often because of two-career households.
- Approaching graduate shortages.

The labour market

The labour force consists of about 2·8 million people, of whom 2·5 million are wage-earners. Of these some 800,000 work in the public sector and 1·5 million in the private sector. In 1989 more than 200,000 members of the labour force were unemployed, equivalent to a rate of approximately 9·5 per cent.

The overall participation rate, at 68 per cent, and the female participation rate, at nearly 60 per cent, are the highest in the European Community. The prevalence of two-career families can make mobility difficult. The labour force grew by an average of 1·1 per cent a year up to the late 1980s, when cyclical factors caused a deceleration to 0·5 per cent. The growth in the labour supply has resulted mainly from the continued growth in female participation, many women being drawn in by the rapid expansion of public services in recent years.

The labour market has strong Nordic characteristics, with a large proportion of part-time workers. With nearly 25 per cent of the work force on part time, Denmark has the second highest rate of part-time employment after the Netherlands.

A great emphasis has been placed on vocational training over the past decade, and in 1987 just under 50 per cent of the labour force completed some vocational training, according to the OECD. The government, trade unions and the employers' organizations have recently finalized the details of an intensive campaign which aims to sustain the number of vocational training places, after a dramatic fall from around 46,000 in 1986 to 33,000 in 1989. An additional 6,000 places are planned. In order to fund initiatives which help to increase the number of trainees in firms, the Dansk Arbejdsgiver Forening (DA), the main employers' organization, has set aside Dkr 10 million (£1 million). The campaign is aimed at larger companies, which currently take on a substantially smaller proportion of trainees than smaller firms. The organizations of employers' in industry, IA, together with the metalworkers' union Dansk Metalarbejderforbund, have set up schemes aimed at creating 8,000 new traineeships in about 30,000 firms in the metalworking industry by September 1990.

Personnel planning

Official notification

Employers have no statutory obligation to report new hirings or quits to the Ministry of Labour or any other organization. The only notification the state receives is through the income tax system. There is no obligation to report vacancies to the official placement system.

Work-force consultation

There are about 3,000 joint workplace 'co-operation committees' in the private sector, established under the provisions of a cooperation agreement between the Danish Federation of Trade

Unions (LO) and the Danish Employers' Confederation (DA). Co-operation committees may be set up in all companies with thirty-five or more employees, provided one is proposed either by the employer or by a majority of the employees. The committee consists of an equal number of members of management and senior executives not eligible for union membership on the one hand, and employees on the other.

The main responsibility of the committees is to promote co-operation throughout the enterprise for the benefit of the enterprise and the individual employee alike. Committees are also responsible for overseeing and improving working conditions as well as ensuring that employees are kept informed about the operations, financial position and competitiveness of the company.

The main objectives of the committees include drawing up the principles of the company's personnel policy and of local working conditions, as well as consultation and co-operation on a range of other issues related to the operation of the enterprise, new technology, and data protection. (The role of co-operation committees in Danish industrial relations will be dealt with in a future volume in this series.)

Co-operation committees are not allowed to discuss any matters relating to industry-level collective agreements or company pay agreements which are dealt with through collective bargaining or conciliation procedures.

The Limited Companies Act of 1974 introduced employee participation at board level so that staff members in companies with more than fifty employees had the power to elect two representatives to the company's board of management. In 1980 an additional provision was introduced to allow a third member to be elected, and the provision was extended to limited companies with thirty-five employees or more.

'Atypical' work

Fixed-term contracts or contracts to accomplish a specific task are permitted. If a contract for less than three months is concluded with a white-collar employee, either party may withdraw without notice, unless explicit agreement has been reached to the contrary. If the contract is for longer than three months, then it will expire either when the task is complete or at the agreed time. Notice of termination in the former case must conform with the law on salaried employees, which provides for one month's notice for contracts for up to five months or three months' notice beyond that, with an additional month's notice for each three years of service, up to a maximum of six months.

Part-time employment is normally covered by collective agreement, and ranges between fifteen and thirty hours a week.

Temporary agencies. Before the recent change in the law on job placement, in force from 1 July 1990, temporary agencies, active principally in the clerical field, were able to operate only with special permission from the Ministry of Labour. However, the new legislation has removed these restrictions, and temporary agencies, including the familiar majors, are now able to operate freely without special authorization.

Finding the applicant

Denmark has recently liberalized its placement system, though its ratification of the ILO Employment Services Convention (No. 88) means that it maintains a free public employment service. The new legislation on job placement activities came into effect on 1 July 1990.

Prior to the new legislation, the state placement service, the Arbejdsformidlingen (AF), had a placement monopoly. Private employment agencies were in general prohibited, but private temporary agencies, particularly in the clerical field, were allowed to operate with the permission of the Ministry of Labour, which was also responsible for the supervision of such agencies. Recognized trade unions were also able to apply to the Ministry of Labour for permission to undertake placement activities within the occupational field covered by the union, and this has traditionally been an important means for the placement of those with academic qualifications.

The new legislation has removed all restrictions from job placement activities and no special permission is required from the Ministry. Trade unions such as Dansk Metal, the metalworkers' union, have now set up a 'job bank' which holds information on employed and unemployed metalworkers, their training, qualifications and details of their present jobs as well as the jobs they are looking for.

The state placement system—Arbejdsformidlingen (AF)

AF is being maintained and under the new legislation it can charge a fee for certain special services but the ordinary services will still be available free of charge. The government believes that the liberalization of placement activities will strengthen the public employment service and increase its efficiency.

The role of the AF, which was set up in 1969, has changed from merely being a placement service to being involved in monitoring, co-ordination and guidance both for the unemployed and for enterprises. This reflected the change in the labour market in the late 1970s and 1980s, when the market moved from a shortage to a surplus of labour with increased levels of unemployment.

However, placement activities and enterprise services remain the chief function of AF. This service provides an analysis of the qualifications and work experience of individual job seekers as well as the qualification and experience requirements of given jobs, and then seeks to match the two profiles. There are approximately 200 public employment offices (job centres) in Denmark, with twenty-eight main offices, of which fourteen are regional offices (one in each county). The AF recruitment service fills about 15–20 per cent of all job vacancies.

AF's role in monitoring the labour market is important in order to detect and avoid demand and supply bottlenecks. The monitoring process is based on close contact between the regional employment services and enterprises. In 1989 about 38,500 inspections of enterprises took place, according to the Ministry of Labour.

Co-ordination of labour market policy initiatives is also provided by AF. This role may also involve co-operation between the municipal authorities and AF regarding measures to combat youth and/or long-term unemployment.

Vocational guidance is provided to job seekers and those seeking educational or training opportunities, and in 1989 AF carried out 358,000 such interviews.

New private agencies

The change in the legislation has enabled various organizations such as trade unions and others to set up a job service. One of the most recent recruitment services has been the Berlingske Job Service (BJS). Set up by the newspaper *Berlingske Tidende*, BJS provides a database service containing a number of members' personal profiles (education, skills, experience, ideas, etc.). It is also a meeting place for qualified job applicants and companies through direct mail. The BJS is aimed at prospective employees aged between 25 and 60 seeking a career, with above-average levels of education and/or experience.

Executive recruitment

There are no particular reported shortages among executive and professional staff, according to the employers' organization DA. However, future shortage in certain areas is expected with the widening of the European employment market. About one in three executives is recruited through advertisements in newspapers and specialist journals, around a quarter of appointments being made through an executive search consultancy, with a higher proportion at board and head of function level.

A number of the European major search companies are represented in Denmark. The Danish Institute of Personnel Management (IP) also maintains an extensive executive recruitment database.

Graduate recruitment is mainly in the form of newspaper and magazine advertisements such as *Berlingske Tidende* for all subjects and sector, *DJØF-bladet* for law and economics graduates, and *Civiløkonomer* for business studies, marketing and economics graduates. Trade unions are also active in graduate recruitment through their journals directed to their student members. Trade unions representing professionals have also traditionally played a role in placing members, and their journals carry job advertisements and placement information.

Most graduates will have completed their nine months' military service, if eligible, before embarking on a job search.

Advertising media

Direct advertising in the press remains the main form of recruitment. *Berlingske Tidende*, the principal business daily, is the prime vehicle, and on its own count carried some 80 per cent of all recruitment advertisements in the private sector and 73 per cent of those in the public sector. *Politiken*, principally the Sunday edition, came second, with 7 per cent of recruitment advertisements in the private sector and 9 per cent of those in the public sector. The business daily *Børsen* is also used for more specialist and senior vacancies.

A Gallup survey of the newspaper reading habits of private-sector employees aged between 18 and 54 looking for jobs carried out in Greater Copenhagen found that 39 per cent of all employees and 56 per cent of those with higher education read *Berlingske Tidende* on Sunday, with 11 per cent and 4 per cent respectively reading the Sunday edition of *Politiken*. *Børsen* was read by 5 per cent of all employees and by 13 per cent of those with higher education.

Specialist magazines also have recruitment sections. For example, *DJØF-bladet* carries recruitment advertisements for staff with a legal and economics background and *Civiløkonomer* which contains a job supplement, 'Jobbørs' for those with a business, marketing and economic background. Specialists can be found through journals such as *Computerworld* or *Ingeniøren* (the joint journal of the two main professional engineers' associations, which has a job section).

Companies cannot specify gender in recruitment advertisements. The general information which is included in job advertisements is typically as follows:

- Company name, and background information, such as turnover, products, branches in Denmark and elsewhere, with locations; exports, if any; number of employees; whether the company is part of a group.
- Age requirements—not always included.
- Specific experience required.
- Salary—not always specified, but benefits and bonuses are often mentioned.
- Detailed job description.
- How to apply for the job.

- Working hours.

Generally, salaries are not specified in recruitment advertisements except for public-sector positions, where a salary range or grade may be given.

Application and selection

The most commonly used procedure of applying for jobs is submission of a C.V. Application forms are not generally used. Some larger companies use aptitude testing or job simulation tests in their selection procedure, with multinationals possibly maintaining assessment centres. The use of assessment centres is increasing, and for a wider range of jobs.

It is difficult to generalize about the intensity of interviewing. The number of times prospective candidates are interviewed varies a great deal between organizations, depending on whether the interview is integrated with other tests, the size and complexity of the company, and the seniority of the position.

Contracts of employment are not a legal requirement. However, their use has been on the increase in the last few years for professional and managerial staff, although still infrequently for unskilled or skilled workers. Managers' contracts are not subject to legislation covering salaried employees, and their contracts tend to be more specific in their terms and conditions. It is quite common for managers to sign a three to five years' contract on appointment.

Work permits. European Community nationals are allowed to work in Denmark without the need for a work or residence permit. Other nationals must apply to the local labour market board through the offices of the state employment service, and permits are usually granted only if no suitable Danish candidates are available.

Quotas and incentives

The disabled. There are no quota requirements for the disabled in the private sector.

Youth employment. The Dansk Arbejdsgiver Forening and the Ministry of Labour have recently launched a youth employment campaign through which state funding is available to employers for the vocational training of young people with a limited education.

Appendix

Organizations

Ministry of Labour
International Section:
19 Laksegade
DK-1063 Copenhagen K
tel. +45 33 92 59 00

Labour Directorate:
Finsenvej 78
2000 Frederiksberg
tel. +45 31 10 60 11

Dansk Arbejdsgiverforening
(Danish Employers' Federation):
Vester Voldgade 113
Postboks 386
DK-1503 Copenhagen V
tel. +45 33 93 40 00
fax +45 33 12 29 76 (publishes a guide to employment in Denmark in English)

Dansk Metalarbejderforbund
(National Metalworkers' Union):
Nyropsgade 38
1602 Copenhagen V
tel. +45 33 12 82 12

Foreningen af Managementkonsulenten
(Management consultants organization—member of FEACO):
Regus House
Larsbjørnsstræde 3
1454 Copenhagen
tel. +45 33 32 25 25
fax +45 33 32 43 70

Publications

Berlingske Tidende:
34 Pilestraede
DK-1147 Copenhagen
tel. +45 33 15 75 75
fax +45 33 93 42 88
London agent: Joshua Powers Ltd
46 Keyes House
Dolphin Square
London SW1V 3NA
tel. 071-834 5566

Børsen:
19 Møntergade
1116 Copenhagen
tel. +45 1 157240

Politiken:
Rådhuspladsen 37
1585 Copenhagen
London agent: Frank L. Crane Ltd
8 Salisbury Square
London EC4Y 8AP
tel. 071-353 1000

Ingeniøren:
DIF/I-S Skelbaekgade 4
1717 Copenhagen V
tel. +45 1 21 68 01
London agent: F. A. Smyth & Associates Ltd
23A Aylmer Parade
London N2 0PQ
tel. 071-340 5058

DJØF-bladet:
Danmarks Jurist- og Økonomforbund
Gothersgade 133
1123 Copenhagen
tel. +45 33 1429 20 (editorial)

Civiløkonomer:
published by
FDC-Danske Civiløkonomer
Vesterbrogade 1 C
1620 Copenhagen V
tel. +45 33 1414 46
fax +45 33 1411 49

3
Recruitment in France

Although the labour market is comparatively highly regulated, employers are largely free to hire whom they choose, and do not have to use the state placement system, although formal notification of vacancies is required. Nevertheless, and in contrast to the UK, areas such as temporary working are subject both to national bipartite agreement and to legislative regulation.

Executive search and the use of recruitment consultants have grown in recent years, reflecting the tighter labour market of the late 1980s for managers and certain types of specialists. Demographic problems are not forecast to be as severe as elsewhere in the European Community, but specific shortages are forecast to persist.

Personnel practitioners in France highlight:

- Shortages of professional engineers.
- A lack of graduates and skilled blue-collar workers.
- Low levels of employee mobility.
- Lack of foreign language skills.

The labour market

The labour force in 1988 stood at 24,153,000 out of a total population of working age of 36,850,000, a labour force participation rate of 66 per cent, compared with 76 per cent in the UK. The participation rate for men was 75 per cent, and for women 56 per cent—up moderately from 50 per cent in 1973, and around mid-place in the European Community. Women now make up 43 per cent of the labour force, compared with some 35 per cent in the mid-1960s.

France's potential work force has been growing by around 0·5 per cent a year during the 1980s, slightly slower than the OECD European average but faster than the UK. Although growth in the 15–24 age population has flattened markedly during the 1980s, and will fall back during the 1990s, rapid population growth during the 1960s means that the overall population of working age will continue to grow at well above the rates expected elsewhere in the European Community during the 1990s. According to Eurostat projections made in 1988, the population aged 15–64 will grow from approximately 37 million in 1990 to 37,770,000 in the year 2000, and to 38,778,000 by 2010. However, by the year 2000 the proportion of that age group aged 45–64 will have increased from 31 per cent to 35 per cent.

Part-time work is still comparatively rare, compared with more northerly European countries: some 11 per cent of employees worked part-time in 1987, compared with 28 per cent in the Netherlands and 22 per cent in the UK. However, compared with southern Europe, where part-time work typically hovers around 4–5 per cent of all employees, the situation is not quite as 'atypical' as might seem at first sight. Nearly a quarter of female employees (22·5 per cent) work part-time, contrasted with just 3·3 per cent of men.

According to the Bureau d'Informations et de Prévisions Economiques (BIPE), the number of jobs requiring graduate skills is set to virtually double, from 5 per cent to 11 per cent of the work force over the period 1982–2000.

Personnel planning

Informing the authorities

All companies with at least fifty employees must make a monthly declaration of new hirings and terminations in the preceding month to the local office of the Ministry of Labour (*directeur départementale du travail*). This does not apply if an employment contract has been agreed for a duration of one month or less. Employers are liable to a fine of Ff 1,300–2,500 for failing to provide the information. All vacancies have to be notified to the state manpower service, Agence Nationale pour l'Emploi (ANPE), whose role is outlined below.

Work-force consultation

Companies are not required by law to consult works councils or employee representatives on the recruitment of individual employees. However, under the Labour Code (Code du Travail, L 432–1), managements must meet the works council in their establishment once a year to discuss the movement of labour within the company over the previous year and to outline proposals and policy for the coming year. Works councils (*comités d'entreprise*) are mandatory in companies with fifty employees or more. The discussion must include part-time and temporary work, and provision for disabled workers.

If works councils request it, companies with fewer than 300 workers must provide information on the movement of labour within the company, together with staff qualifications, atypical working and training programmes, not less than twice a year. Companies with more than 300 employees must provide this information, if requested, not less than three times a year (Labour Code, L 432–4).

Collective agreements do not contain provisions on personnel planning but frequently impose requirements on recruitment procedures and priority for internal candidates.

Using part-timers and temps

Part-time working is legally defined as any employment of four-fifths or less of either the statutory working week (thirty-nine hours) or the appropriate collectively agreed working week.

Contracts for part-time employees must be in writing, and specify the number of hours to be worked: any changes in working hours must be notified to the employee at least seven days in advance. Overtime may not exceed one third of the agreed working time and must not increase the part-time employee's hours beyond the statutory or collectively agreed limit. Part-time workers are entitled, on a pro-rata basis, to all benefits enjoyed by their full-time colleagues and are given priority of consideration for full-time vacancies if they so wish.

Works councils or employee representatives need not be consulted in the case of individual part-time appointments, but consultation must take place on the general principle of part-time working in a company or if the proportion of part-time workers in the company changes significantly. Full-time employees have the right to refuse to change their working hours on to a part-time basis at the request of the employer.

The use of *temporary staff* has increased over the past few years, with this sector representing 7 per cent of the total work force in 1989 compared with 2·5 per cent in 1977. This trend has prompted the government to propose legislation aimed at regulating temporary work, and in particular to limit the use of temporary, rather than permanent, staff to fill vacancies. The Bill was adopted by the National Assembly and the Senate on 12 July 1990 and is now law.

Its main effect will be to:

- Define more tightly when an employer may have justifiable recourse to temporary staff (such as short-term increases in work load, seasonal work and urgent work in order to prevent accidents).
- Limit the total length of a temporary contract (renewable once only) to eighteen months.
- Increase temporary employees' entitlement to training and unemployment benefit.
- Prohibit companies from taking on any temporary staff in the six months following a dismissal for economic reasons.

According to the union of temporary workers, Promatt, there are some 230,000 workers in temporary employment at any given time. It also estimates that, owing to the high number of people entering and leaving temporary employment, some 900,000 people will have worked on a temporary contract every year. Temporary work may be a springboard to permanent employment in some cases: a year after the first study sample, 20 per cent of participants had found a permanent job, 48 per cent were still in temporary employment, 22 per cent were on fixed-term contracts (*contrats à durée determinée*) and only 8 per cent were unemployed. The national statistics institute, INSEE (Institut Nationale de la Statistique et des Etudes Economiques), found that around half of people employed on fixed-term contracts and a third of those on temporary contracts were in permanent employment a year later.

Temporary contracts are drawn up between the agency and the employee and must be in writing, setting out terms and conditions and a possible trial period. A separate written contract must exist between the user company and the temporary employment agency, stating the reasons for recourse to temporary work, the duration of the assignment, a job description and the agreed pay.

The central organization for temporary work agencies is UNETT (Union Nationale des Entreprises du Travail Temporaire).

Employees have rights *vis-à-vis* both the agency and the user company. For example, the employee has a right to be paid at least twice a month by the agency. Temporary employees are not deemed to be employees of the user company, but they must be entered into the company's register of personnel movements. They are also entitled to all normal company benefits for employees, such as advice from workers' representatives.

Temporary employees are currently entitled to an end-of-contract bonus of 5–15 per cent of gross salary, paid by the temporary employment agency. As from 1 November 1990 a flat rate of 10 per cent for temporary employees and 6 per cent for employees on fixed-term contracts will be introduced as a result of the new legislation (see above). Employees on temporary and fixed-term contracts are also entitled to sick pay (50 per cent of gross salary for the first thirty days and 25 per cent of gross salary for the following forty-five days) on production of a doctor's certificate and provided they have 670 hours of general experience, 360 of which must be with the present agency during the preceding twelve months. Maternity benefits are also payable (at the daily rate of one 360th of gross salary earned during the previous twelve months for sixteen weeks) to those employees with either 1,600 hours of temporary work experience in the twenty-four months preceding maternity leave or 670 hours of experience with one temporary employment agency.

There are statutory obligations which a temporary employment agency must meet, both when setting up and whilst in operation. Any agency wishing to begin an operation must make a written declaration of intent to the labour inspectorate (L 124–10, R 124–1). The agency is also obliged to submit a report to the local office of the Ministry of Labour as well as the local branch of ANPE, the state job placement agency, of all contracts concluded each month. There are penalties for not concluding a **written** contract with either the user company or the employee, or if an agency has drawn up an employee contract which does not set out the full terms and conditions of employment. User companies can be penalized for unauthorized recourse to temporary employment, unlawful renewal of contracts, not having a written contract with the agency or preventing the access of temporary workers to staff facilities, such as works canteens.

Finding the applicant

Agreed provisions

Before embarking on recruitment, companies need to know whether or not they are covered by any collective agreements—either national or at industry level—which require them to follow some set procedures or limit what they can and cannot do during the recruitment process. Some examples are set out below.

In distribution and retailing, vacancies must be advertised internally to give existing staff priority and the terms, conditions and proposed pay rate must be set down in writing.

In chemicals, employers must inform interested parties, such as other employees, of general staff needs across all grades and inform the works council of any appointments, apart from temporary and seasonal workers. Where employment levels fluctuate markedly, priority in hiring should be given to any employees terminated in the previous twelve months because of lack of work. Age must not be a discriminatory factor in making appointments. All appointments have to be confirmed by letter or other written notification, and new employees have to be given a copy of the company agreement and the relevant collective agreement.

In metalworking, the appointment of managers and specialists must not be limited by age. All newly hired employees must be given written confirmation, with a job description, of pay, hours and the place of work. A letter of appointment may not contain any limitation on an employee's trade union activities. Employees have fifteen days in which to query the contents of the letter, after which their agreement is assumed.

In hotels and catering, existing employees have preference for newly arisen vacancies. Any employee terminated for economic reasons during the previous twelve months also has priority, but this is forfeited if the first offer is rejected, or if no **reply is made** within eight working days. All employees must receive written confirmation of employment. A 'technical test' may be required for certain jobs, but it may not last for more than one day. Any test lasting longer than two hours is paid for by the employer at the minimum rate for the grade.

The state placement system

The state job placement system ANPE (Agence Nationale pour l'Emploi) provides recruitment services for blue- and white-collar workers and managerial staff.

Employers wishing to recruit externally may use ANPE or registered private employment agencies. ANPE possessed a monopoly of placements until legislation passed in 1986 (No. 86-1286) enabled other organizations to make placements provided they had an agreement with ANPE. These organizations include public bodies such as chambers of commerce and bodies which are jointly controlled by employer and employee organizations, such as the executive placement organization APEC (see below).

Nevertheless, all vacancies must still be notified to one of ANPE's local regional offices, with fines ranging from Ff 600–1,300 (£60–£130) for failure to comply. Similarly, all workers seeking employment and who want to receive unemployment benefit need to register with ANPE and renew their registration regularly, although this is not legally enforceable. In areas where there is no regional office, the town hall (*mairie*) must be notified of vacant posts. On employing an ANPE-registered worker an employer must notify ANPE within forty-eight hours. Employers are not bound to employ workers recommended by ANPE, and, similarly, workers are not obliged to accept job offers made by companies through ANPE.

ANPE provides services to people looking for a job as well as companies looking for staff. The agency will also carry out some pre-selection and testing of candidates.

A total of 1·2 million job offers were made via ANPE in 1989, an increase of 9·7 per cent over the previous year, with permanent jobs accounting for 56 per cent of this total. Managerial placements fell by 18 per cent, some of which may be attributable to the increased use of private agencies and consultants. In 1989 ANPE filled 70 per cent of the 310,000 vacancies notified to it for unskilled and semi-skilled workers and routine white-collar jobs, 55 per cent of the 713,000 vacancies for skilled blue- and white-collar jobs, and 37 per cent of the 54,000 managerial and supervisory vacancies. ANPE claims to fill vacancies within fifteen days for 70 per cent of the first category, 84 per cent of the second and 80 per cent of the third. However, only 9 per cent of companies turn to ANPE for managers, as there is a specialist state placement service for executives.

ANPE's efficiency and ability to cope with the volume of placements required and requested have been the subject of a good deal of employer criticism in recent years. The organization is undergoing a major overhaul which will be completed in 1993.

The state executive placement service. The state executive placement organization, APEC (Association pour l'Emploi des Cadres), provides its services free to users and is financed by charges levied on employers for each employee registered in the state executive pension scheme ARRCO (Association des Régimes de Retraites Complémentaires) amounting, on average, to 0·06 per cent of gross salary. This is supplemented by a lump sum payable by employees and employers once a year which varies according to the ceiling on social security contributions. The amount in 1989 was Ff 75.20 for employers and Ff 45.12 for employees. APEC made around 8,500 managerial placements in 1989.

According to a study carried out by APEC itself, and based on the recruitment practices of some eighty companies, 37 per cent of companies used APEC for finding middle managers, 21 per cent for senior managers and 23 per cent for new executives. The main user companies tend to have 200–300 employees.

Recruitment consultants

Recruitment consultancy has taken off in France over the past few years, and is currently growing at 10 per cent a year, a rate of growth likely to be sustained with increased job mobility amongst executives: an estimated 200,000 managers now change jobs each year. Newspaper advertising by consultants was up by nearly 17 per cent in 1989 compared to the previous year.

According to APEC, consultants place around 16 per cent of all executives recruited. An analysis of job offers published by consultants gives the most popular sectors as computing and general commercial, with 17 per cent and 33 per cent of all jobs advertised, respectively. The average processing time for recruitment requests is estimated at five to seven weeks for recruitment by advertisement and eight to twelve weeks for recruitment by direct approach.

The usual fee charged by consultants is around 20 per cent of annual salary for a placement using advertisements, 25 per cent of annual salary for a placement using a mixture of advertisements and direct search, and 30–35 per cent of annual salary for search only. If a selected candidate leaves the job within a year of recruitment, consultants will generally look for a replacement free of charge.

The professional body for consultancies in France is SYNTEC, which has 122 member companies operating in the field of recruitment. SYNTEC members operate to a code of professional ethics centred on the client–consultancy relationship. A full copy of the code of conduct and a list of members can be obtained from SYNTEC. SYNTEC is a member of FEACO, the pan-European trade organization for management consultancies (for FEACO's address see page 177).

There are currently some 100 firms specializing in executive search and selection, handling 3,500–4,000 searches a year. Just under a half of these are for top-level management. Search firms are legally obliged to keep a public record of their computerized filing and retrieval system. The method of recruitment depends primarily on the salary offered for a particular job, jobs with annual salaries in the range of Ff 120,000–300,000 (£12,500–£30,600) being advertised, jobs with salaries in the range of Ff 300,000–600,000 (£30,600–£61,000) being advertised together with a search operation, and jobs with salaries over Ff 600,000 (£61,000) using search only.

The central organization for executive search consultancies is APROCERD (Association Professionelle des Conseils d'Enterprise pour la Recherche des Cadres). APROCERD members are expected to work to a code of conduct on assignments which requires that:

- Consultants may accept business only from companies or organizations looking for managers, not individuals looking for work. Individual advice must be provided free of charge and only occasionally.

- Consultants may accept only assignments they feel qualified to fulfil satisfactorily, which must be agreed with a written contract with the client.
- The professional obligation of the search consultant is that of providing an efficient service to the best of their ability, and is therefore an obligation of effort, not of results.
- Fees must be established by written contract at the beginning of the assignment on the basis of scale, difficulty and duration.
- Assignments should be carried out solely by direct approach to persons or organizations.
- Consultants are bound to secrecy unless instructed otherwise.
- Consultants should not recontact candidates already placed by themselves as long as that person remains with the company in which placement took place, and should not contact employees of former clients for a period of two years.
- Consultants should refuse all non-exclusive assignments and should refuse all unofficial methods of payment.

A full copy of the code of conduct and a list of member companies can be obtained from APROCERD.

APROCERD also recommends a recruitment approach to its members which should consist of:

- Identification of potential candidates and contact.
- Confidential interview with candidates.
- Presentation of selected candidates to clients.
- Assessment of candidates' employment history, with candidates' permission.
- Assistance in final negotiations.
- Follow-up assistance in integrating the chosen candidate into the new employment.

Direct recruitment

Advertising. Any company wishing to advertise a vacant post in the press must supply the company name and address to the newspaper should they wish to remain anonymous in the advertisement. ANPE and the local labour department, or the Paris department if the advertisement appears in a national newspaper, must also be notified of vacancies.

Advertisements must not contain:

- An upper age limit.
- Knowingly false or misleading statements about the nature of the employment, the salary or the place of work.
- Discriminating statements on the grounds of race, religion or sex.
- Any foreign expressions or words if a French equivalent exists. If no French equivalent exists, then an explanation of the term in French must also be given. Exceptions are granted when the place of work will not be on French soil, when the advertiser is particularly seeking applicants from one country, or if the advertisement appears in a foreign-language journal.

Penalties for contravention of these restrictions range from Ff 600 to Ff 1,300 (£60–£130).

Advertisements for managers in the press are increasing. According to a study by APEC, around 98,000 posts were advertised in 1989, an increase of 17 per cent over the previous year. In response to the still buoyant computing market, the largest single category was posts in the computing sector (25,282), although the largest increase was seen in the research sector ('études, recherches, projets'), with 11,982 posts, up 43 per cent on the previous year. Conversely, advertisements for jobs in production and manufacturing have slumped over the last decade, with a decrease of 25 per cent between 1980 and 1989. Most of the advertisements were for posts in the Paris region (54·2 per cent), confirming the central role of the capital for managerial positions.

For technicians, supervisory staff and specialist staff, *Le Figaro* and *France-Soir* are the main carriers of advertisements; *Les Echos*, the business daily owned by the Pearson Group, and *Le Monde* share the market for financial, managerial and administrative positions. Four-fifths of computing posts are advertised in the specialist journal *01 Informatique*. Engineering jobs are mainly to be found in *L'Usine Nouvelle* and *Le Moniteur*. Personnel positions are mainly advertised in *Liaisons Sociales*, whilst *L'Express*, *Le Point*, *Le Monde* and *Le Figaro Economie* carry advertisements for senior managers.

Recruitment by radio. There are a number of radio programmes on which companies can advertise vacancies and invite listeners to apply. One example, the programme *Challenge*, is broadcast on France Inter at 8.15 each morning. Some private stations also have a similar service, with prices ranging from Ff 1,800 a spot to Ff 5,700 for twelve spots.

Poster advertising. This is not a widespread method of recruitment but it was tried successfully by Spie-Batignolle in 1988 when it advertised for staff on 1,800 posters and received 3,000 telephone calls and 1,200 letters.

Using Minitel. The computerized information service Minitel, which can be accessed from the home through a television screen, is now used regularly by an estimated 30 per cent of French households, and can also give help to both job seekers and employers.

If a Minitel number is given when a post is advertised in the press, potential candidates can obtain further information via the system about the company and the advertised post. The candidate may then do a short 'pre-selection' test devised by the company that placed the advertisement, which, if they pass, gives access to more details, such as the name and telephone number of who to contact about the post. This is an inexpensive method of pre-selection and can save time and money for both employers and candidates by weeding out the utterly unsuitable at an early stage without direct involvement by the company. Minitel is accessed within France through the telephone and television network by means of a special installation.

Research carried out by Minitel shows that out of 100 candidates accessing information about an advertised post, sixty do the pre-selection test, twenty-five are pre-selected and ten actually go ahead and apply for the job. Some consultants and job placement agencies such as APEC can also be accessed via Minitel.

Graduate recruitment

According to a survey carried out by the magazine *L'Etudiant* and published in its annual guide on recruiting companies (see appendix), speculative letters from potential candidates constitute the largest single method through which graduates and young employees are recruited. The survey, based on replies to questionnaires from companies operating in France on their methods of recruiting graduates, found that, in order of frequency, the main methods cited by the 221 participating companies were: speculative letters from potential candidates; advertisements; work experience placements (*stages*); associations of former students; recruitment consultants; and headhunters.

The survey also lists the main graduate recruiters and starting pay for graduates by sector and educational background. The top ten companies in terms of the number of graduates taken on each year in 1989 were as follows: Thomson, 1,600; Cap Sesa, 1,000; Banques populaires, 950; Sema Group, 700; Télésystèmes, 610; Matra, 600; Aérospatiale, 550; Cisi, 550; France-Télécom, 550; Renault, 550.

Recruitment practice varies for graduates, depending on the type of higher education establishment. The *grandes écoles*, the most prestigious and more vocationally oriented degree awarding institutions, usually have both developed counselling and placement offices as well as active societies of former students. Although most universities—whose degrees are not as accepted by French employers as directly relevant to business—have careers information offices, their placement activities are not as highly developed.

Recruitment fairs are organized each year by a number of technical colleges and higher education establishments, where companies set up shop to provide graduates with details of themselves and their vacancies. The cost varies, depending on the type of educational establishment. The number of recruitment fairs has increased over the past couple of years.

Large-scale recruitment events have also developed in recent years, and details of the main fairs can be found in the journal *L'Usine Nouvelle*, which publishes a list each November. Fairs can be expensive and need to be booked in advance.

The following recruitment fairs have been identified as among the main recruitment events by the UK graduate recruitment researchers ATS Quest: Job Salon (Paris, 5–6 October 1990: general); Supélec (Paris, 5–6 December 1990: engineering/general); Rhône-Alpes (Lyon, 6–7 March 1991: engineers); Convergence 91 (Paris, 19–20 March 1991: science/technology); Forum ESCP (Paris, April 1991: business/general).

APEC can also be used to find graduates (see above).

The average salary graduates can expect in their first job depends both on sector and on educational background. Graduates tend to be assessed very much by the educational institution attended, rather than by details of academic performance, which anyway are not readily accessible to employers. Figures from the *L'Etudiant* survey illustrate the range. Average starting salaries, in order of type of degree, were Ff 163,000–179,000 for graduates of the top business schools (the Ecole des Hautes Etudes Commerciales, the Ecole Supérieure des Sciences Economiques et Commerciales and the Ecole Supérieure de Commerce de Paris), and Ff 146,000–167,000 for graduates of other business schools; Ff 166,000–184,000 for graduates of the leading engineering schools (Polytechnique, Centrale, Mines, Ponts, Télécom, Supélec, ENSAM, Sup'aéro and Agro) and Ff 152,000–171,000 for graduates of other engineering schools; for those completing a four-year university course, Ff 148,000–165,000 and for those completing a five-year course Ff 141,000–157,000.

Educational background remains a strong influence throughout an employee's working life, especially for those in top managerial positions. Graduates of the *grandes écoles*, which strictly limit their annual intake, receive on average five or six job offers on graduating, according to the business magazine *L'Expansion*, and in mid-career earn on average 45 per cent more than graduates of universities or technical colleges.

Application documents

Employers are not allowed to include questions on application forms about union membership, political opinions, religious convictions, family situation or pregnancy.

There are no statutory restrictions requiring employers to seek the permission of candidates before submitting their applications to graphology tests. This practice is widespread in France and is often contracted out to graphology experts by companies and sometimes even by recruitment agencies.

References are taken up in 70 per cent of managerial recruitments carried out via consultants. However, this rarely applies to academic references.

The type and amount of information which can be legally gained about a prospective employee is limited under article 9 of the Civil Code, under which all persons have the right to respect for their privacy—an employer has no right to enquire into an employee's private life except when it is deemed relevant to the proper operation of the employer's business. Under law 78–17, the collection, storage and distribution of personal information by computer are regulated, and companies wishing to start up a database must notify the National Commission on Freedom of Computerized Information (Commission Nationale de l'Informatique et des Libertés). No persons, excepting next of kin and legal representatives, are allowed access to the personal identification numbers issued to all French citizens. Certain types of financial information, such as bankruptcies, are available in public registers, but the disclosure of information which would be obtainable only from a bank is a violation of article 378 of the Criminal Code. Public records, tax and property archives may be consulted by the public only seventy years after the date of the relevant entries.

Selection

Methods

Employers are free to choose their means and methods of selection. Psychological tests may be used, but the employer is not legally bound to make the selection according to the results.

According to APEC, the recruitment process for a manager in France typically involves: sorting C.V.s and first weeding out of applicants; a further sorting, often using graphology, leading to the second round of elimination; candidates may then be tested, followed by the third round of elimination; interviews precede the fourth round, and may be followed by a second graphological analysis, the checking of references, contact with the previous employer and then a final interview.

The *L'Etudiant* survey asked its 221 participating companies to list their main methods of selection. The methods and the number of companies using them were: graphology, 69; personality test, 46; two interviews, 19; three interviews, 38; four interviews, 33; five interviews, 11; six interviews, 2; intelligence test, 16; group interview, 10; job simulation test, 5.

Graphology is used by an estimated 80 per cent of consultants, according to APEC, both to pre-select candidates and, more widely, to 'verify' the impression derived from an interview. Psychometric testing seems to have lost credibility among personnel managers and has declined in popularity over the past fifteen years. Personality and intelligence tests are used widely, especially by consultants. There is no statutory obligation to inform candidates of the results of the tests, although some consultants do.

Our research also found reports of firms and consultants using palmistry, astrology, phrenology and haemotology to assess the character of candidates and their compatibility with existing employees.

Privacy

Under the Labour Code, article L 123–1, reference to the sex or family situation of a candidate is prohibited when making an offer of employment or in any publicity relating to recruitment. It is also illegal to refuse employment on the grounds of sex or family situation. These restrictions apply not only to the employer but also to any organization involved directly or indirectly in the recruitment process, such as employment agencies or newspapers.

Employers may ask candidates about their civil status, military obligations, qualifications and professional history, and may request certain documents, such as exam certificates, employment certificates and, if applicable, letters of dismissal, but only if they are deemed directly relevant to the proposed employment. For example, it is permissible to ask a candidate about school performance and examination results, as they may give an indication of competence for the job, but not to request a school report, as it might contain private information concerning the social and family circumstances of the candidate.

Candidates have the right to withhold information or give *incorrect* answers, if they feel that an employer is asking inappropriate questions, without prejudice to their subsequent employment rights.

Employers are allowed to ask candidates about a possible criminal record only if it is directly related to the position applied for, such as where the post involves the handling of large amounts of money or the security of premises or persons.

Medical examinations. All employees are required to have a medical examination before an appointment (R 241–8) and, if applicable, before the end of the probationary period of employment. The purpose of the examination is to ensure that a prospective employee is fit enough to do the job in question. If an employee does not prove to be fit enough, the employer may offer a different post, although this is not obligatory. Medical examinations are not necessary if the employee has already been examined when being appointed to a similar job during the preceding six months (the period is increased by twelve months if the job is with the same employer).

Employees are required to have a further medical examination once a year, or whenever requested by the employer. A refusal by the employee to undergo medical examination could constitute grounds (*cause réelle et sérieuse*) for dismissal.

Employment incentives

There are a number of government incentives designed to increase general employment or to encourage employers to take on certain categories of worker. The main incentives are listed below.

As from January 1989 the government introduced exemption from the payment of social charges for employers taking on their first permanent employee, for a period of two years. This offer was taken up by a total of 70,000 employers in 1989. Employers are also exempted from the payment of social charges (for a period of nine months) if they take on a registered unemployed person or a person receiving the statutory minimum income (RMI) under a 'return to work' scheme (*contrat de retour à l'emploi*, or CRE) and receive a one-off bonus payment of Ff 10,000 (£1,020). Some 8,400 of these schemes were in existence in 1989.

Young persons

Various schemes aim to encourage companies to train and give work experience to young people aged between 16 and 25. The three main training courses (TUC, Travaux d'Utilité Collective; PIL, Programme d'Insertion Locale; AIG, Activités d'Interêt Générale) do not involve any payment of wages by the employer (trainees are paid either by the state or by the social security organization, ASSIDEC), nor is the employer liable to any social security contributions. A solidarity contract (CES) is designed to follow on from the initial training contract. The employee is paid the national minimum wage (SMIC), 85–100 per cent of which the employer can claim back from the state, which will also help with any training costs. These contracts have a minimum duration of three months and a maximum of twelve months.

Women

In order to encourage companies to employ more women and to comply with the 1976 EC directive on professional equality, the government has created two incentive schemes, the 'Plan pour l'égalité professionnelle dans l'entreprise' (occupational equality plan) and 'Contrats pour la mixité des emplois' (equal opportunity contracts).

The occupational equality plan may be drawn up on a company basis and would typically include things such as reserving a recruitment and promotion quota for women and having training schemes for women only. If the government approves the plan, employers are entitled to reimbursement of up to 50 per cent of the training costs incurred, up to 50 per cent of other costs incurred and up to 30 per cent of salaries paid during the training period.

The equal opportunity contracts are aimed specifically at small and middle-sized companies with fewer than 200 employees, and aim to promote the interests of individual female employees through training and improving working conditions and the working environment: this includes reducing the amount of physically demanding work or fitting extra showers and cloakrooms. Employers are entitled to reimbursement of up to 50 per cent of training costs, up to 50 per cent of other costs and up to 30 per cent of salaries paid during training.

Disabled workers (*travailleurs handicappés et mutilés de guerre*)

There are legal obligations on some companies to recruit a certain number of disabled staff. Companies employing at least twenty-five staff must employ a number of disabled staff equivalent to not less than 5 per cent of the total work force. This proportion will be increased to 6 per cent in 1991.

Companies may apply for various state subsidies available for employing the disabled. They include: financial aid of up to 80 per cent of the cost of modifying work tools or the working environment in order to improve disabled access, and up to 50 per cent of any additional costs incurred; aid of up to 80 per cent of the current value of the national minimum wage (SMIC) and the cost of employer social security contributions if an employer takes on a disabled worker on a professional training scheme (*contrat d'adaption professionnelle*); a company is eligible for aid of Ff 20,000 per disabled employee recruited (up to a maximum of Ff 750,000) if the company concludes a 'professional integration contract' (*contrat d'insertion professionnelle*) with the state. Under such a contract, which is valid for three years, the employer takes on a number of disabled workers, equal to a minimum of 4 per cent of the company's work force, guarantees these employees a certain amount of professional training, and agrees to contract out a programme of work to sheltered centres for disabled people and occupational therapy centres. Works councils must be notified of all plans to apply for these contracts.

A number of agreements concerning the recruitment of disabled workers have been concluded at sectoral level. For example, the national electricity and gas industries (EDF–GDF) signed a three-year agreement in November 1989 which pledges the annual recruitment of a number of disabled workers equivalent to at least 1·5 per cent of the overall level of recruitment—this will amount to around 140 persons a year.

Long-term unemployed (*chomeurs de longue durée*)

State aid is available to encourage companies to take on a long-term unemployed person aged 26 or over, on a fixed-term or permanent basis. These contracts (*contrats de réinsertion en alternance*), must provide the beneficiary with a period of training which, if the contract is fixed-term, must total a minimum of 300 hours, up to a maximum of half the total length of the contract. Employers are exempt from social charges for these employees and are entitled to state aid towards training costs.

Military service

If requested by the employee, a company must make every effort to reinstate an employee who has been engaged in military service and who used to work for the company. If it is not possible, the employee is entitled to priority of reinstatement for the period of one year. Military service lasts for one year—students usually choose to undertake it after graduation. Military service may be replaced by a slightly longer period of voluntary civilian service.

Making the offer

There is no set procedure which employers are required to follow when making an offer of employment. However, most companies would prefer to have a written record of a job offer. A letter offering a job may be used to constitute a contract of employment (*lettre d'engagement*), in which case it should clearly set out the employee's grade, pay, hours, other main terms and conditions of employment, and the place of work.

Handling rejection

There is no statutory formula for handling the rejection of unsuccessful applicants. However, as with offers of employment, rejections tend to be in writing.

The average time taken by companies to process job applications varies, according to the *L'Etudiant* survey, from two weeks to four months. APEC also found considerable variation, depending on the size of the company, with faster processing of applications in smaller enterprises. More than half of companies with 500–2,000 employees took over two months. Taking all companies, 70 per cent had completed processing within two months.

Not all applicants accept the offer, of course. APEC found that only a quarter of companies had all their offers accepted, but just over 80 per cent of firms had 80 per cent of their offers accepted.

Work permits and papers

Employees are usually required to present employers with their identity card, exam certificates and, if they have already been in employment, their social security registration card and a certificate of employment from their previous employer.

A distinction is drawn between EC nationals and other foreign workers. EC nationals must have an EC national residence permit if they wish to work in France (*carte de séjour de ressortissant d'un état membre de la CEE*), which must be obtained in the three months following arrival in France (decree No. 81–405, free circulation of workers within the Community). Until 1 January 1993 the situation is slightly different for Spanish and Portuguese nationals, who are required to obtain a work and residence permit before taking up employment. When the permit expires they are eligible for an EC national five or ten-year permit.

All other foreign nationals must obtain a residence permit (*titre de séjour*) and a work permit (*titre de travail*) before taking up employment. If the nature of the employment is permanent, both permits can be incorporated into one card. Temporary residence permits are valid for one year (*carte de séjour temporaire*). Longer-term residence permits are valid for ten years (*carte de résident*) and can be obtained only by foreigners who are married to a French national, who have immediate members of family who are French nationals or who have been living in France for at least three continuous years.

Employers are responsible for checking that an employee has a valid residence and work permit and are liable to a fine of Ff 2,000–20,000 (£200–£2,000) or imprisonment of two to twelve months for contraventions.

Appendix

Organizations

Ministry of Labour:
127 rue de Grenelle
75700 Paris
tel. +33 1 40 56 60 00

Association pour l'Emploi des Cadres (APEC):
51 boulevard Brune
75689 Paris Cedex 14
tel. +33 1 40 52 20 00
fax +33 1 45 39 10 22
APEC also has regional offices, including Marseille (address:
APEC Marseille
229 avenue du Pocado
BP 352
13271 Marseille Cedex 08
tel. +33 91 91 79 32 52)
and in Lyon
(APEC Lyon
204 avenue Bethelot
69361 Lyon Cedex 07
tel. +33 7 78 69 04 77)

Agence Nationale pour l'Emploi (ANPE):
23 rue Felix
Paris 75009
tel. +33 1 49 31 74 00

Confédération Générale des Cadres (national executives' union):
30 rue de Gramont
75002 Paris
tel. +33 1 42 61 81 76

Conseil National du Patronat Français (national employers' organization):
31 rue Pierre 1er de Serbie
Paris 75016
tel. +33 1 40 69 44 44

SYNTEC (member of FEACO):
3 rue Léon Bonnat,
75016 Paris
tel. +33 1 45 24 43 53
fax +33 1 42 88 26 84

APROCERD (search consultants' organization):
120 avenue des Champs-Elysées
75008 Paris
tel. +33 1 44 20 54 00

Promatt (union of temporary workers):
94 rue Saint-Lazare
75009 Paris
tel. +33 1 48 78 11 21

UNETT (national organization for temporary employment agencies):
9 rue du Mont-Thabor
75001 Paris
tel. +33 1 42 97 41 50

British Chamber of Commerce:
8 rue Cimerosa
75118 Paris
tel. +33 1 45 05 13 08
fax +33 1 45 53 02 87

Publications

Le Monde:
1 place Hubert-Beuve-Méry
94852 Ivry-sur-Seine Cedex
tel. +33 1 49 60 32 90

Les Echos:
46 rue La Boétie
75381 Paris Cedex 08
tel. +33 1 49 53 65 65
fax +33 1 45 61 48 92

Le Figaro:
25 avenue Matignon
75398 Paris Cedex 08
tel. +33 1 42 36 79 19

Le Point:
140 rue de Rennes
75066 Paris
tel. +33 1 45 44 39 00

Le Guide des Entreprises qui Recrutent:
(annually costs Ff 98.00, available for different levels of education)

L'Etudiant (regular journal):
27 rue du Chemin-Vert
75543 Paris Cedex 11
tel. +33 1 48 07 41 41
fax +33 1 47 00 79 80

L'Usine Nouvelle:
59 rue du Rocher
75008 Paris
tel. +33 1 43 87 37 88

Liaisions Sociales:
5 avenue de la République
75541 Paris Cedex 11
tel. +33 1 48 05 91 05

Code du Travail
(Labour Code):
Editions Dalloz
11 rue Soufflot
75240 Paris Cedex 05

4
Recruitment in Germany

The labour market in Germany has been redefined, and profoundly transformed, by the process of economic, social and political unity between the two German states and the migration of ethnic Germans from Eastern Europe and the German Democratic Republic. This will have a direct impact on employers intending to recruit staff, in terms of both the number and the type of applicants looking for work. The newcomers will alter both the age and skill profile of the work force, relieving some but by no means all of the concerns about the drying up of the supply of school and university leavers in the 1990s, and later on fears of the impact on social security systems of a rapidly ageing population. At the same time, the development of an employment service in the five new eastern *Länder* of a united Germany poses a fearsome challenge, given the scale of unemployment and the need for massive retraining in many occupations.

Nevertheless, despite this influx of new workers, and despite the persistent pool of unemployed workers, skill shortages are expected to continue into the 1990s, given continuing economic growth and the expected structural changes in the work force which will reflect Germany's relatively belated development as a service-dominated economy.

Students study for longer than in the UK, and PhDs are more common than in British industry. British companies recruiting in Germany will find a highly skilled work force, with a deeper level of training experienced by a larger proportion of the work force, including clerical staff, than in most other European countries. In 1987 nearly 60 per cent of the work force had completed a course of vocational training, 11 per cent had a higher education qualification, and only 23 per cent had no vocational training at all.

Employment legislation can be complex, and has not been codified. Special attention needs to be devoted to the requirements of the law in areas such as consultation and co-determination with employee representatives, especially for managers coming from a more informal background. However, the requirement to consult employee representatives on personnel planning or rigidities in labour law were not rated as a major problem by employers, compared with other aspects of the labour market. These included:

- The falling number of school leavers.
- Skill shortages in general, and of graduate engineers in particular.
- Low inter-regional mobility.

This chapter is based on recruitment law and practice as applicable in the Federal Republic. Although many requirements of Federal labour law and many Federal institutions, including the job placement system, have been, or will be, transferred to the former Democratic Republic, both formal and cultural differences will remain, especially as regards terms and conditions of employment.

The labour market

Two major processes are currently shaping the labour market: the slump in the number of young people, and the effects of German unity and the immigration of ethnic Germans from Eastern Europe. The net effect of this inward migration of an estimated 3·7 million people between 1990 and the year 2000 into the former territory of the Federal Republic will offset much of the lower birth rate of the late 1970s, and increase the population of the former west by some 3·1 million. This compares with the fall from 61 million to 60 million forecast by Eurostat in 1988.

Migrants from the GDR (*Übersiedler*) tend to have higher skills than ethnic Germans from Eastern Europe, 80 per cent of whom arriving in 1989 did not have a full command of German.

Despite this medium-term addition to the potential labour supply, many sectors have recently been concerned about skill shortages, with particular problems reported in the construction, electrical engineering and chemical industries, and with small and medium-sized firms harder hit than large companies.

Employers have attributed the problem both to training policies and, especially in the engineering industry, to the cuts in working hours effected since 1984. In contrast, the trade unions have contested the view that there is a generalized shortage of skills.

The effects of the slump in the number of school leavers are already being felt in the form of a surplus of training vacancies over applicants: in the period October 1989 to June 1990 employers had a total of 620,000 training vacancies, for which there were only 410,000 applicants, a drop of nearly 6 per cent on the previous year, with reported shortages of applicants in manufacturing-oriented apprenticeships.

The female participation rate in the Federal Republic's western *Länder*, according to the OECD, is around 54 per cent, about the average for other OECD European countries. Female participation rates in the five new *Länder* in the east are much higher: in 1988 83 per cent of working-age women were in employment in the German Democratic Republic, compared with 82·4 per cent of men.

Part-time work, which accounts for approximately 13 per cent of the work force, is around the EC average.

Personnel planning

Consulting the authorities

Employers must obtain the appropriate residence and work permits, and ensure that employees are insured in the state pension and unemployment benefit system and against occupational accidents, as well as registered for tax purposes. A list of the requirements is set out before the appendix.

The factory inspectorate (*Gewerbeaufsichtsamt*) must be informed when pregnant women are employed. There are also registration requirements on the employment of the severely disabled. However, there are no other requirements to inform the labour authorities when hiring.

Consulting the work force

There is a statutory obligation to consult works councils and seek their agreement in a number of areas connected with recruitment and appointment, including:

- Personnel planning.
- Internal advertisement of vacancies.
- Application documents.
- Guidelines for employee selection.
- Appointments.

Each of these is dealt with at the appropriate point in explaining the recruitment process.

Under the 1972 Works Constitution Act (*Betriebsverfassungsgesetz*) works councils may be elected by the work force of any establishment with at least five eligible permanent employees: certain types of establishment are exempt if they serve scientific, educational, artistic, charitable, political or religious ends, or if they are concerned with journalistic reportage or the expression of opinion.

Future volumes in this series will deal with the full rights, responsibilities and structure of works councils and their role in the system of industrial relations. Works councils have a number of legally enforceable rights to information and codetermination across the spectrum of employment and personnel management in an establishment, and in some areas—notably termination of employment—any action taken by managers without notifying the works councils could be regarded as null and void.

Under legislation passed in 1988, where there are at least ten executives in an establishment, they may elect an Executive Representation Committee (*Sprecherausschuß*) which will have the right to be consulted on a number of areas affecting managers' employment, pay and conditions. Executives do not count as eligible employees for the purposes of the legislation under which works councils operate. The definition of 'executive' includes such aspects as the right to hire or dismiss staff and the level of salary.

On personnel planning, article 92 of the Works Constitution Act obliges employers to *inform* works councils 'in full and in good time' about current and future demand for personnel, any resulting staff movements and training implications, and to back this up with the 'relevant documentation'. Employers must also *consult* works councils on the nature and extent of any action required, and means of avoiding hardship to employees. Works councils can make recommendations on the introduction and implementation of personnel planning.

The notion of 'personnel planning' is relatively broad, covering not simply any systematic and quantitative assessment of future staff needs over the long term but also company responses to immediate situations where they involve an element of planning. Setting up a personnel information system would also mean consulting the works council.

Works councils can request that all vacancies, or vacancies for certain positions, should be advertised internally before external recruitment begins and can refuse to agree to a new hiring if no internal notification has been given. (Works councils' rights in this area are dealt with in the section on making appointments, below.) However, the employer and works council can conclude a works agreement—which is then binding on both parties—to exclude certain types of job from advance internal notification.

A number of collective agreements, including metalworking and banking, also require that 'due account' should be taken of the wishes of any existing part-timers who want to change to full-time work.

Using part-timers and temps

The use of fixed-term contracts—both directly and via temporary work agencies—has grown enormously in recent years, aided by the easing of some of the legal obstacles by the 1985 Employment Promotion Act (*Beschäftigungsförderungsgesetz*). This piece of legislation sets out the framework within which such 'atypical' areas of work as fixed-term contracts, part-time employment, job sharing and 'work on call' or 'capacity-oriented working hours' can be agreed.

Employees with less than six months' service or in an establishment with five or fewer eligible employees are not covered by the provisions of the 1969 Protection against Dismissal Act (*Kündigungsschutzgesetz*), which sets conditions related to the employee's conduct or person, or requires economic grounds, for a dismissal to be lawful.

Fixed-term contracts can be agreed between the employer and a potential employee if there is a 'material reason' why the contract of employment should not be indefinite: such reasons would include a task limited by its nature in time, such as seasonal work, artistic performances, research projects **constrained by** funding, or to meet a temporary employment need such as filling in for an employee absent through illness. Unless otherwise agreed, a fixed-term contract can be terminated only when the agreed period has elapsed, except for misbehaviour sufficiently serious to warrant summary dismissal. Under the 1985 Employment Promotion Act, which will remain in force until 1995, a fixed-term contract may be agreed *once* for up to eighteen months without the need for a material reason, either with a new employee, or with someone who has just completed vocational training and for whom no permanent post is available. This period is extended to two years if the employer started the business less than six months previously, or if the employer employs ten or fewer employees, excluding trainees. A succession of fixed-term contracts may be concluded without a material reason with an employee provided there is a gap of at least four months between the end of one period of employment and the beginning of the next.

Part-time work is defined as any employment involving working hours less than those worked by full-time employees in an establishment. Some collective agreements specify minimum hours. Part-timers working less than fifteen hours a week and earning less than DM 470 a month are not subject to sickness and pension insurance contributions. Part-timers working less than nineteen hours a week are excluded from unemployment insurance and benefits. However, employers are liable for the employer and employee social insurance contributions of employees earning between DM 470 and DM 620.

'*Work on call*', known in Germany as 'capacity-oriented variable working time' or by its acronym, KAPOVAZ, requires employees to work when requested to do so by the employer. (Such arrangements are sometimes termed 'zero-hours contracts' in the UK, though this is a misnomer in the German context.) Such arrangements must specify a certain number of working hours: if this is not agreed, then a minimum of ten hours per week will apply, which the employer has to pay for. Employers must give at least four days' notice of any period of work.

Temporary workers can be found through private temporary work agencies and via the state job placement system. The state temporary work service, administered by the Federal Employment Institute, provides employees for fixed-term employment with an employer, under the conditions for such contracts set out above. The Job temporary personnel service places clerical and sales staff in fixed-term posts of up to three months. The Servis temporary work service arranges the placement of very short-term blue-collar jobs in ports, markets and trade fairs. The service is free to both employers and employees. Details of the state placement system as a whole are set out below.

Authorized *temporary work agencies* are allowed to supply workers to firms on a temporary basis subject to the regulations of the 1972 law on commercial employment agencies (*Arbeitnehmerüberlassungsgesetz*). The major international providers of temporary staff which operate in the UK can also be found in Germany. There are approximately 1,300 firms engaged in the provision of temporary workers as their prime commercial activity. About 400 agencies employ more than fifty agency employees. Agency employment is forbidden for manual workers in the construction industry.

Employees are employed by the agency, not the client, and the agency is responsible for the payment of wages, tax and social insurance contributions, and must ensure that employees receive paid holidays and sick pay, even if they are not working for a client company. A written contract must exist between the agency and the client, and it must indicate whether the agency is officially authorized.

Employees may not work on the premises of a client company for longer than six months at a stretch, and there are other limits on the amount of time agency workers can work for one client as a proportion of their total employment with an agency.

Agency staff do not count as part of an establishment's work force in the calculation of the number of works council delegates. Works councils have a right to be informed of an employer's intention to use agency workers.

Agreements which do not allow a client to engage agency employees who have terminated their employment with the agency—that is, which forbid poaching of agency staff—are null and void.

The Bundesverband Zeitarbeit (BZA) serves as the central organization for eighty-five authorized member companies **employing just** over 100,000 workers, out of a total **of around**

300,000 employed in this area of the market annually. The BZA has a code of conduct for member companies, and had a framework collective agreement with the white-collar union DAG, which is not affiliated to the main union federation, the Deutscher Gewerkschaftsbund (DGB). Although the agreements have expired, and were not renewed, their provisions remain in force. The DGB is generally hostile to temporary work. The BZA's minimum conditions for member companies include four weeks' paid holiday a year and contributions to travel costs. The BZA forbids members to make staff available to companies whose work force is lawfully on strike.

The Schutzgemeinschaft Zeitarbeit e.V., established in 1987, also represents a number of major agencies, and issues a 'seal of approval' to firms which meet what it regards as more stringent conditions than those required by the BZA. Member companies must give 24 days' holiday a year, and pay annual and other bonuses, and have a three-year trouble-free record with the authorities which gives them indefinite official authorization.

Employers in the same branch may also 'lease' workers to each other on a non-commercial basis if allowed to by collective agreement, and subject to notification of the authorities. Such arrangements can be used to meet labour shortages if another undertaking in the same branch has a temporary surplus of workers and 'leasing' out the surplus will avoid redundancies. Since January 1990 firms with fewer than twenty employees suffering economic problems may 'lease' workers to other firms which are members of the same local chamber of commerce without official permission, though they must notify the labour authorities.

Subcontracting is permitted on the basis of a 'contract of service' between a subcontractor (or individual) and an employer where the job is aimed at a definite objective or result, and where the subcontractor retains the supervision of the employees on the premises of the client: subcontracted employees may not become involved in the regular operations of the client company. Remuneration must be related to the fulfilment of the objectives, and may not be on the basis of hours worked.

Finding the applicant

The state placement system has a monopoly. No organization is allowed to undertake job placement or provide career counselling—that is, operate as an employment agency—for a consideration, but non-profit-making organizations may do so on application to the authorities. Although the authorities have been prepared to agree guidelines permitting private consultancy in executive recruitment, and more recently to be more flexible in their attitude to private agencies in the arts, they are committed to their monopoly in the permanent placement of the vast bulk of employees. A more flexible attitude is also adopted to events such as recruitment fairs, where career advice and placement may be outside official channels. However, newspapers and periodicals are allowed to accept advertisements from employers and notices from work-seekers and both companies and work-seekers are free to find each other directly. The management consultants' organization BDU is currently challenging the official placement monopoly in the European Court.

Breaches of the law on placement may entail a fine of up to DM 30,000 or, in cases of the placement of foreign employees without work permits and on conditions widely disparate from those of German nationals, imprisonment for up to five years.

The Federal employment service

The Federal employment service is run by the Federal Employment Institute (Bundesanstalt für Arbeit, or BfA), whose headquarters are in Nuremberg. The BfA is a self-governing organization incorporated under public law and operating in accordance with various statutory provisions, the most important being the 1969 Work Promotion Act (*Arbeitsförderungsgesetz*). All the management bodies of the BfA are composed in equal numbers of representatives of employees' organizations, employer organizations and public bodies. By tradition the president of the BfA is a member of the political party in government, the vice-president a member of the opposition.

The BfA offers a wide variety of services, free of charge, to both employers and work-seekers, including:

- Placement.

- Training.
- Career counselling, including a school and college leaver service.
- Occupational health care, including capacity rating for the disabled and the obligatory examination of young persons entering employment for the first time.
- A psychological service, which tests about 190,000 people a year.
- A technical advisory service.

The service operates through nine regional employment offices and nearly 150 local employment offices. (The central address of the BfA is to be found in the appendix.)

Employers can inform their local or any other employment office of vacancies in writing or by phone, fax or telex. If the office is unable to find a suitable candidate immediately, it will try to suggest other options.

Candidates will be offered by the employment office on the basis of their suitability and individual circumstances. However, in certain circumstances preference will be given to specific categories of protected employee, such as the disabled, where candidates are otherwise equally suitable. In accordance with anti-discrimination legislation, the BfA will not pursue requests for only men or only women to fill a vacancy: it will suggest equally suitable male and female applicants, subject to protective legislation or where gender is relevant to the job.

There is no obligation on an employer to accept candidates proposed by the state system, and the terms of a contract of employment are a matter for the two sides alone, subject to the law, jurisprudence and any relevant collective agreements.

Since 1988 an experimental vacancy information service known as SIS (Stellen-Informations-Service) — akin to UK Job Centres — has been running in some regional employment offices, and will probably be extended to the whole country. Under SIS all the vacancies on offer in a local labour office are set out on a computer terminal or in a list with details of the employer, and job seekers can approach firms direct without going through the full placement procedure.

The BfA also offers a specialist service for employers needing temporary staff, for companies needing staff for trade fairs, and for finding short-term employment for students. The details are set out in the sub-section dealing with temporary employment above. Employment and training incentives are also administered and financed via the BfA: details are set out separately below.

The service also produces a large number of publications, including a weekly free newspaper, *Markt + Chance*, which is published in two editions: edition A contains individual presentations by job seekers, and edition B advertises registered vacancies. These are available from local employment offices.

In addition to its placement-related services, the BfA administers the unemployment benefit system, the payment of child benefit, occupational rehabilitation, the collection of labour-market statistics and research.

The service is generally well regarded, and much used for blue- and white-collar positions and specialists, although less so for senior managers. There have been recent employer criticisms that it cannot cope with the volume of demands placed on it, and innovations such as SIS are intended to raise the capacity of the state system. In 1989 nearly 2,300,000 placements were made, of which just over 60 per cent were in permanent positions. Around 30 per cent of placements were in temporary positions of less than six months. In all, approximately a third of all vacancies on the labour market are offered for placement to the state service, and in 1988 it accounted for approximately a quarter of all those newly entered into contracts of employment lasting longer than seven days. The success rate, measured as the ratio of placements to offered vacancies, is around 70 per cent: the average time taken to make a placement in 1989 was 22·5 days—although the BfA hopes that the influx of workers from the GDR will widen the supply of skills and enable it to cut the time to twenty days, the norm during the 1980s.

Managers and specialists

Newspaper advertisements remain the most common form of recruitment where managers and specialists are concerned: details of the main publications are set out below. Direct approach is also a common, but so far somewhat covert, method, recently legitimized by a new set of guidelines for consultants.

One increasingly important forum in which employers pursue managerial and specialist talent is the major trade fairs, to which companies frequently send personnel managers and recruitment teams equipped with customized literature to talk to potential applicants. The larger fairs may have career centres which job seekers can visit. Of particular importance in areas beset by skill shortages are:

- CeBIT, the information technology and telecommunications fair held annually in Hanover.
- The international motor show (IAA) in Frankfurt.
- The Hanover Industry Fair.
- Drupa (printing and paper) and IGEDO (fashion) in Düsseldorf.
- Systems and electronica (computers and components) and Bau (building materials) in Munich.

Details of the main trade fairs, with costs, can be obtained from the Confederation of German Trade Fair and Exhibition Industries (AUMA).

As well as major employers, most of the large personnel—that is, recruitment—consultants also attend the main fairs: both frequently place advertisements in the major newspapers inviting applicants to their stands. Often firms which have no direct link with the trade in question but feel a need to be present wherever qualified job seekers are around also book space.

The state placement service for managers and specialists. The state placement system includes a special service covering managers and qualified specialists, centred on the Central Placement Office (Zentralstelle für Arbeitsvermittlung, ZAV) in Frankfurt. A number of large cities with universities also have specialized offices for the placement of those with academic qualifications and managers, known as the Specialist Placement Services (Fachvermittlungsdienste, FVD). All local offices of the FVD are on a common computer network and linked with the ZAV.

The ZAV's and FVD's services include:

- Information on executive labour markets, both generally and by sector and function.
- The development of job descriptions and identification of potential applicant groups: direct contact with managers on the ZAV's books.
- The formulation and placing of advertisements.

- Systematic search for, pre-selection and presentation of suitable candidates.

Information on current vacancies can be obtained through the German teletext system on Btx * 6 91 00 22 #.

Managers on the ZAV's books are not necessarily unemployed: in fact two-thirds of candidates who approach the ZAV for career counselling and possible placement are in employment and not working out notice.

Specific departments within the ZAV deal with national management placements and international placements, broken down by sector, with the specialist departments for placement within Germany broken down both by level of responsibility (departmental head or top management) and by broad function, and within that by sector. As well as the private sector the ZAV also makes placements in the public sector, with a specific department handling medical staff.

There are also specialist services in Frankfurt and other regional employment offices for entertainers, film crews, hotel staff, qualified agricultural staff and sailors.

The ZAV has sixty specialists working directly with applicants and firms and in 1989 made some 3,000 placements directly, although only about 600 were management placements within Germany. Some 975 out of the total were of foreign managers and specialists looking for employment in German undertakings. Thirty-six per cent of placements were in health care, 40 per cent in industry and 24 per cent in commerce or services. Just over half of all placements involved salaries of DM 100,000–140,000 p.a., with 20 per cent above this figure: twelve placements involved salaries over DM 300,000 p.a.

The 'specialist placement system' (FVD) handles about 170,000 applications a year nationally from individuals with university or higher-level vocational qualifications. In 1988 it placed 30,000 individuals in response to 40,000 registered specialist vacancies, of which 7,000 were engineers.

All the ZAV and other specialist services are free to employers and applicants alike. Advertisements may be placed in the press but only on the instructions of individual companies, who are invoiced direct by the publisher.

Recruitment consultants

In 1988 advertisements placed by recruitment consultants—which as explained below are termed 'personnel consultants'—in national newspapers accounted for just over 40 per cent of all advertised managerial positions, and around a quarter of all managerial and specialist positions combined, with a rising trend.

The official state placement and counselling monopoly has left consultants in a position of legal uncertainty, although agreements with the BfA have allowed them a reasonably free rein in the field of executive search and selection. New guidelines agreed between the consultants' organizations and the BfA in July 1990 have eased some of the previous restrictions limiting executive search operations.

The guidelines establish a demarcation between placement—which consultants are not allowed to practise—and the provision of advice to client companies on recruitment. Consultants must confine their advice to the appointment of executives and high-level specialists, who are more precisely defined in the agreement. The consultancy must be offered to a client within the context of a broad assignment, and may include:

- Analysis of vacancies.
- The development of a job profile and establishment of the criteria sought in an applicant.
- Search, pre-selection and presentation of qualified applicants.
- Advice in setting pay and other terms and conditions.

Fees must be either fixed or payable on the basis of the consultant's time on the assignment: contingency fees are not permitted.

A consultant may undertake a single assignment, provided the overall recruitment process remains under the supervision and direction of the client. The new guidelines allow direct approach subject to some constraints.

- Poaching 'contrary to good ethics' or with the intention of impairing free competition is not permitted.
- The same executive can be repeatedly approached on different assignments only with the target employee's permission.
- The consultant may not raid a small company's entire

management in order to meet one, or several simultaneous, assignments.
- 'Unrealistic' salary offers may not be made.
- Covert approaches, under the guise of conducting business, for example, are not allowed.
- Consultants must respect any managers' express request not to be approached.

Consultants are not permitted to engage in placement as such, and could face prosecution for contravening the guidelines. Placement may be deemed to have taken place if a consultant:

- Looks for potential candidates without working on a specific assignment.
- Retains a candidate's application documents (theoretically rendering it illegal to maintain and develop certain types of database).
- Acts on behalf of an employee—although outplacement is permitted.
- Demands a contingency fee from employee or client.
- Publishes advertisements on behalf of a client but which give the impression that the consultancy effectively operates as a recruitment agency.

Executive and professional search and selection are carried out as an activity of personnel consultants, many of whom are more broadly management consultants, although specific search companies—including most of the large internationals—do operate. There were around 800 personnel consultancies in 1988, employing 2,000 individual consultants and with a total fee income of some DM 1 billion. The two main organizations for personnel consultancies are the relevant professional section of the management consultants' organization, the BDU (Bund Deutscher Unternehmensberater), known as the 'Fachgruppe Personalberatung', and an organization specifically for personnel consultants, the Arbeitskreis der Personalberater in Deutschland. Details of both organizations are given in the appendix. The BDU publishes an annual list of its member companies, setting out their services and specialisms, and is a member of FEACO.

Personnel consultancies which are members of the BDU are subject to two codes of practice—one as management consultants, and a further code covering their specific activities in the personnel field.

The general code is a voluntary one, but BDU member companies commit themselves to settle disputes arising out of the code before an arbitration tribunal. Although most of its requirements relate to general professional conduct and competence, confidentiality and fee practices, there is a specific clause on poaching (*Abwerbung*) which obliges companies not to induce employees to leave clients, either for employment with the consultancy or with a third party, and forbids the employees of consultants to open discussions with a client about possible employment. BDU members are also forbidden to poach from each other. Restrictive covenants can be agreed in Germany, and companies may use the courts to ensure that they are adhered to: this issue will be dealt with in a subsequent volume in the series.

Companies in the BDU who wish to join the personnel consultants' section must agree to abide by a specific code of conduct. Its main requirements are:

- A commitment to high professional standards in the conduct of consulting assignments as regards suitability for the task and the recommendation of solutions, a striving for continuous improvement, a commitment to a high level of knowledge of the executive labour market, and a high level of competence in the use of all selection techniques.
- A commitment to confidentiality as regards client and candidate alike: no information about a candidate may be passed to a client nor may references be taken up without the candidate's permission.
- Consultants must be equally objective in their advice to both clients and candidates; positions must be realistically and fully described, and candidates' abilities and characteristics described and evaluated for clients.
- Clear agreement must be reached on fees and expenses. Contingency fees may not be agreed.
- Member companies engaged in executive search will participate as consultants in filling a managerial vacancy only if they are exclusively engaged by the client.
- Member companies may not seek to find employment for a candidate and may be engaged by client companies only for a specific assignment; they may not request a fee or a consider-

ation from candidates, operating not 'as "candidate brokers" or intermediaries but as problem solvers through consultation'.

Certain aspects of fee practice are regulated in the rules set down by the Bundesanstalt für Arbeit. The cost of an executive search is typically 30–35 per cent of the annual remuneration involved.

Recruiting graduates

Recruiting graduates in the 1990s is likely to be more difficult than in the late 1980s, when the 'baby boom' years of the late 1960s led to a flood of school leavers and graduates. As the demographic squeeze tightens, a changing employment structure will raise the demand for qualified people.

According to forecasts of the labour market carried out jointly by the employment research section of the BfA and the consultancy Prognos, highly qualified jobs will account for 39 per cent of the work force by 2010, compared with 28 per cent in 1985, implying an absolute growth of nearly 3·5 million workers in this category. By the year 2000 15 per cent of the work force are expected to have university-level qualifications, compared with 10 per cent in 1985.

'Secondary services'—which cover such sectors as research and development, organization and management, teaching, consultancy and the caring professions, are expected to expand from 5·7 million workers in 1985 to 7·7 million in 1995, and to 9·2 million by 2010.

At the same time the number of people in the 20–24 year age group is expected to decline by around 40 per cent between 1990 and 2000, on the basis of forecasts prepared for the former Federal Republic alone.

Higher pay and better immediate prospects will no doubt lead to a continuing net movement of qualified people, including graduates, from East into West Germany. There will be transitional problems related to the quality and assessed equivalence of East German qualifications in the West, and graduates from East German universities are more likely to be assessed on their general ability rather than specific vocational skills. The Federal Vocational Training Institute (Bundesberufsbildungsinstitut) has been working on the equivalence of qualifications and in 1990 published a guide setting out the two systems and rating vocational qualifications.

Graduates and career-starters in Germany are older than is usual in the United Kingdom, and this to some extent explains higher graduate starting pay in Germany. A German student with a first degree is on average nearly 28 years old, compared with 22 in Britain. The reasons are principally:

- Later school starting and leaving ages, with school pupils sometimes required to resit years.
- Military service of fifteen months or civilian service as an alternative for conscientious objectors lasting twenty months: about one in eight of those conscripted opt for civilian service. Military service is likely to be cut to twelve months from late 1990, with an equivalent cut in civilian service, as a result of the dramatic changes in the military situation following unity.
- Longer period of studies. The average for German students is seven years, compared to an average of four in the UK.

The prospect and reality of graduate shortages, exacerbated by strong economic growth since 1988, has prompted many employers to devote greater energy and resources to the search for graduate talent, encapsulated in the notion of 'personnel marketing'. The main methods of graduate recruitment are:

- Newspaper advertisements, including the use of specialist journals detailed below under 'Using the press'.
- Company visits to campuses, including seminars and presentations. So-called 'contact exchanges' (*Kontaktbörse*) for visiting companies are often organized by student unions.
- Recruitment fairs and general trade fairs. In 1990 the personnel managers' organization, the Deutsche Gesellschaft für Personalführung, organized graduate recruitment fairs (*Karrierebörse*) in Düsseldorf and Wiesbaden at which (mainly larger) firms made presentations, and intends to develop the service in the future. Other major recruitment events for university graduates include the fairs organized by the *Forum* organization, based in St Gallen, Switzerland. Student-run organizations and AIESEC-affiliated student unions also organize recruitment fairs. Details of trade fairs are set out above.

- Direct contact with students, former students and academics.
- Contacts established through training placements, degree dissertations, or organized visits to factories by students.

The methods by which companies first establish contact with students have been researched by the twice-yearly career handbook *Karriereführer* in a survey carried out in 1990. The study, which looked at students at *Fachhochschulen*, degree (or diploma)-awarding institutions of higher education with a stronger vocational bent and broader entry requirements than universities, concluded that:

- Nearly 90 per cent of companies used advertisements.
- Around 80 per cent encountered students during industrial placements: these are a part of a *Fachhochschule* course, but many university students also seek placements during vacations as a way of contacting firms.
- Just under 70 per cent of employers cited contact through degree dissertations (*Diplomarbeit*) carried out by students, especially in commercial or technical subjects, in a business context.
- Over half of all employers encountered students at trade or recruitment fairs.
- Just over half the firms first contacted students who were doing vacation jobs on their premises.
- Nearly two-thirds of firms maintained contact with academic staff.

According to a survey carried out by the Deutsche Gesellschaft für Personalführung (DGFP), average starting salaries for graduates by field of study in 1989 ranged from DM 76,000 (£25,763) a year for a graduate chemist at the top of the scale to between DM 60,000 and DM 64,000 for university graduates in economics, sociology or psychology, information technology, mechanical and electrical engineering; graduate lawyers and a university-educated Diplom-Kaufmann on average earned DM 58,000–59,000.

The largest single group of graduates in the survey, mechanical engineering graduates of *Fachhochschulen* (25 per cent of the sample), earned on average DM 53,500 in the first year of employment.

Within each specialism, starting salary depended broadly but by no means solely on age and length of period of study. Among the graduate chemists, who accounted for a tenth of the DGFP sample, starting pay ranged from DM 58,000 up to DM 89,000 for a PhD aged 34 with a total of twelve years' study.

The expected length of study to first-degree level would be six years for one of the engineering professions and five and a half for an economist.

Other factors bearing on pay—and employability—cited by local practitioners include:

- Specific subject combinations.
- Examination grades.
- Languages—with English a must for management trainees, and a second European language highly desirable.
- Computer literacy.
- For technical professions, a vocational training qualification, such as a completed apprenticeship, before higher education.

Using the press

Press advertising is widely used for all categories of employees, including managers. However, German newspapers are highly regional, with few truly national papers. Nonetheless, some essentially regional quality papers have developed a wider and in some cases an international readership. Specialist journals are also well developed, and offer an option for particular specialist employees, such as engineers or computer specialists.

For blue-collar, clerical and administrative positions the dominant vehicles are regional and local newspapers, too numerous to list here. These newspapers can also be used for managerial and special positions. In many instances, regional newspapers or groupings have a considerably larger circulation than more nationally available qualities. Details of the main supra-regional papers and regional press are set out in the appendix.) Local offices of the Bundesanstalt für Arbeit could advise on the most appropriate local media.

For managers and highly qualified specialists the main newspapers are:

- The daily *Frankfurter Allgemeine Zeitung (FAZ)*, which has national coverage.
- The daily *Süddeutsche Zeitung (SZ)*, which has national coverage as well as local sections for Munich, where it is based.
- *Karriere*, a supplement for executive and specialist recruitment, which is published in the weekly business magazine *Wirtschaftswoche* and on Fridays in the business daily *Handelsblatt*.
- The national daily paper *Die Welt*, which has a north German focus.
- The Sunday national *Die Zeit*.
- The daily *Frankfurter Rundschau* (*FR*), which has national coverage and specialist sections for the Frankfurt (Rhine–Main) area.

The fact that there are a number of quality dailies (*SZ, FAZ, FR*, etc.) with a strong regional focus but a national readership does have the advantage that an employer is likely to be able to attract applicants from within the local area as well as to reach motivated readers nationally. In general, regional employee mobility in Germany is relatively low.

Engineers can be looked for in the journal of the engineers' professional association (Verband deutscher Ingenieure, VDI) *VDI-Nachrichten*, as well as *Der Jung-Ingenieur*. Computer specialists can be looked for in the weekly magazine *Computerwoche* and electronics specialists in *Markt und Technik*, also published weekly. Specialist journals are highly developed, and many carry job advertisements. Details can be found in *Willing's Press Guide*.

There are also some specific journals aimed at graduates and career starters, such as *Absolventen-Zeitung*, *Allgemeiner Hochschul-Anzeiger* and *Junge Karriere*, published as part of the 'Karriere' supplement in *Handelsblatt* with longer special issues twice-yearly. *Süddeutsche Zeitung* also has an occasional supplement for graduates and young managers entitled 'Hochschule und Beruf'. The Bundesanstalt für Arbeit publishes *Markt + Chance* which lists both vacancies and work seekers.

The Civil Code (article 611 b) forbids employers from advertising vacancies for men or women only, unless the gender is an indispensable prerequisite. Although publication of a non-gender-neutral advertisement is not in itself grounds for a claim for damages from a potential employee, it could be read as an indication of a discriminatory intention which would give a rejected candidate stronger grounds for a claim: the possible damages are dealt with in the section dealing with discrimination on appointment. The requirements of German grammar dictate the ways in which this can, or has to, be achieved in German-language advertisements.

Age limits may be specified. Salary ranges are almost never indicated in newspaper advertisements for managerial or other posts, including blue-collar ones.

Vacancies at all levels are typically advertised under the company name, except where a personnel consultant is undertaking a selection exercise. Otherwise, anonymity could be viewed as disguising a company with problems. The perceived greater competition among companies for a diminishing pool of graduates is also stimulating firms to concentrate on presentation and content in the design of job advertisements.

Application documents

Most applicants, and especially those for senior or specialist jobs, would be asked to provide full, and backed-up, personal and professional details, including:

- A handwritten letter of application.
- *Curriculum vitae.*
- School, work or educational and training records, including placements for graduates, and leaving certificates (*Zeugnisse*). Employees have a right to such a certificate from their employer, indicating the major elements of the C.V. and, at the employees' request, an assessment of their conduct and performance in their previous employment. According to case law, the contents of a *Zeugnis* must be true and must not unnecessarily inhibit the occupational progress of the employee.
- A photograph.
- An application form/questionnaire from the company.

Where a company wishes to use an application form (or staff questionnaire for existing employees), the approval of the works council must be obtained, if there is one. If the parties cannot agree as to the content of the form, the matter can be resolved by a binding ruling from a conciliation committee established under the 1972 Works Constitution Act.

The invitation by an employer to work seekers to apply for vacancies, and the sending in of application documents, in themselves create a 'quasi-contractual relationship' which imposes a certain requirement on the employer to keep application documents safe, not to divulge the information in them to anyone without a direct interest in the recruitment process, or to pass application documents as a whole on to a third party. Other mutual rights and obligations are entered into by each party as to the information which can be asked for and which may, or need not be, supplied by the applicant. We examine these issues in the section dealing with selection and with making the offer.

There is no legal requirement to confirm receipt of an application. However, candidates are entitled to ask for the return of application documents if the employer takes an unreasonably long time in dealing with the application—what counts as reasonable depending on the seniority of the position.

Should the application fail, the applicant is entitled to the return of all documents except the formal letter of application. The employer may not make copies of the documents without the express permission of the applicant.

In obtaining information from applicants, either by an application form or through an interview, employers have the right to seek information and expect a truthful answer, on areas relevant to the prospective employment but may not ask questions which encroach upon applicants' private lives or which seek to obtain information which is not relevant to their capacity to perform the advertised tasks. What this means in practice for the conduct of an interview is dealt with below under 'Selection'.

Data protection is a major issue—evidenced by recent controversy about the conduct of the Federal-wide census—and care must be taken to ensure that the handling of information on employees conforms with the requirements of the 1977 Federal data protection law (*Bundesdatenschutzgesetz*) and the 1972 Works Constitution Act. Individual employee rights and employers' obligations in this area are set out in detail in a forthcoming volume in the series.

Once employed, individuals have the right to examine files

held on them, and to append their own observations if they wish. There are general limitations, elaborated by the Federal Constitutional Court in 1984 on the issue of the national census, on what types of data may be collected and stored electronically, when they must be deleted, and who can have access to the information. Although these principles are not directly applicable to employment, prevailing opinion holds that the court's decision, together with other individual rights at the workplace based on the Works Constitution Act, has created normative conditions which give individuals rights over data held on them, and especially their transfer and how long they may be stored.

Selection methods and procedures

Selection guidelines

Any guidelines established by employers for the selection of employees have to be approved by the relevant works council. If no agreement can be reached, the employer may apply for a ruling to a conciliation committee established under the Works Constitution Act.

In establishments with under 1,000 employees, employers are free to choose whether or not to set out explicit guidelines: if they do so, works council approval is required. In establishments with over 1,000 employees the works council can ask for guidelines to be drawn up, and if no agreement is reached with the employer the council can ask for a binding ruling from a conciliation committee.

Such guidelines can establish what occupational, personal, social or other factors are to be taken into account in selecting applicants, together with their relative priority and weight. They could include such factors as formal education, work experience, family size and tested ability during the selection process. Works councils also have a right of co-determination over any principles of appraisal, both for applicants and for existing employees, which an employee may wish to introduce.

Where an Executive Representation Committee (ERC) exists the employer and the committee can agree written guidelines on the commencement and termination of executives' contracts.

Such guidelines will be directly binding on contracts of employment but may diverge in favour of the individual manager.

Selection methods: rights and obligations

The interview, followed at a distance by the aptitude test, remains the most common and central selection technique, with other methods—such as psychometric tests—lagging some way behind. Assessment centres may be used for more senior appointments or for graduate starters. Employers using interviews, or other methods, need to be aware of some of the constraints set by law which also guide practice.

The employer's right to seek information on which to make a hiring decision is constrained, in broad terms, by articles 1 and 2 of the Federal basic law—the constitution—which guarantee the inviolability of individual dignity, the development of the personality, and the inviolability of the person. These underlying principles have been developed by the courts as establishing a personal sphere on which outsiders—including employers or those appointed by them, such as private investigators—may not encroach. Some legal opinion holds that applicants do not have to give truthful answers to impermissible questions if a truthful answer might prejudice the likelihood of being hired: they may answer incorrectly without prejudice to themselves if appointed. In any event, only an untruthful answer to a permissible question is generally held to be grounds for termination.

Employers must give the applicant accurate information about the nature of the job, and especially any associated health risks or requirement to undertake particularly demanding tasks, travel extensively, and so on. There is no obligation to give details of the business, unless the ability of the employer to meet the terms of the contract—that is, pay wages—is in question.

Employers must ensure that they do not arouse expectations on the applicant's part of being certain to get the job before the material and legal prerequisites have been met. Should an employee give notice to their present employer on the basis of such expectations, the prospective employer could be found liable for civil damages.

Applicants' expenses for attending an interview are borne by the employer: in certain circumstances an applicant may be able to obtain a grant for application and interview costs from the Federal Employment Institute.

Interviews may include only questions which are relevant to the job. However, because much of the law in this area has evolved through court decisions, it will not necessarily cover every eventuality, be clear and unambiguous, or be directly applicable to the individual instance, where a different combination of factors might apply. Interviewers may not ask about membership of a political organization, or about the political orientation or school of thought of the applicant's educational institution or teachers. There is some doubt about whether an employer can ask about trade union membership, but the predominant view is that it is impermissible if the intention is to assess the applicant's desirability for employment. An employer may not require an individual either to leave or to join a trade union as a condition of employment.

Interviewers may need to exercise care in questioning an applicant about previous employment where it might involve the disclosure of commercial confidences.

Questions about previous, as opposed to desired, salary are generally impermissible where it is of no relevance to the current position: this could apply for junior posts, but previous income would be likely to be regarded as relevant for senior jobs. The principle also applies to broader questions about an applicant's financial circumstances.

In general, questions about the applicant's health may only seek information about current illnesses which might reduce their ability to meet the requirements of the position either at present or for the foreseeable future, set against the reasonableness of any financial burden on the employer. Applicants are obliged to inform prospective employers about any factors in the state of their health which could reasonably be expected to be decisive in the employer's decision. There is no obligation on the employee to divulge information about illnesses which have occurred in the past and which have no relevance to the employee's future capacity.

The question of employer and employee rights on the issue of AIDS is still uncertain. Prevailing opinion takes the view that a test to establish HIV status is impermissible, except for a position, such as established civil servant, involving life long tenure. However, it would be permissible to ask whether an applicant is suffering from an acute stage of AIDS, and conversely someone in that condition would be obliged to inform a prospective employer. Simply agreeing to a blood test as part of a medical examination does not imply consent to a test to establish HIV status, and any such test would require an applicant's express agreement.

The law on asking about *pregnancy* has evolved within broader considerations of sex discrimination which are also dealt with below. In 1986 the Federal Labour Court ruled that employers may not in general ask a female applicant whether she is pregnant unless all the applicants for a vacancy are pregnant or the job involves tasks which a pregnant woman may not perform under maternity protection provisions. Under certain circumstances the applicant would be under a general obligation to inform a prospective employer about pregnancy if it would be a major impediment to the proposed occupation. Applicants may not be asked about their marriage plans.

Enquiries about an applicant's *criminal record* can be directed only at offences relevant to the proposed employment: this may vary according to the nature of the job and the degree of trust required. Applicants do not have to inform an employer about offences which are no longer on record in the Federal register of convictions (and hence recorded in an official police certificate of conduct, *Führungszeugnis*) because they are deemed to be minor or where the conviction is spent. Some legal opinion holds that employers may not ask an applicant to present such a record of conduct as a condition of employment, as it could contain information not directly relevant to the vacancy.

Medical examinations are typically requested by companies, usually carried out by a doctor working on the employers' premises or appointed by them, and must be paid for by the prospective employer. Applicants must answer questions truthfully. The doctor may not inform the company of the details but only say whether the applicant is fit or unfit for the employment.

People beginning employment in the food industry must first be examined by the official department of health (Gesundheitsamt). Drivers of passenger-carrying vehicles must be examined by a recognized occupational physician.

Companies wanting to employ young people under 18 must ensure that they have been medically examined in the previous nine months, unless the job is for less than two months and entails only light duties.

The consent of the applicant is required for *graphological or psychometric tests*. Simply sending in a handwritten letter of application does not in itself imply consent. Moreover the questions or the characteristics explored must be relevant to the proposed employment, and the degree of incursion into the applicant's personal sphere will vary, depending on the seniority and character of the job.

In the case of psychological testing, it is recommended that occupational psychologists subject to the confidentiality requirements of the Penal Code (article 203) are used.

Anti-discrimination provisions

Under the Federal basic law no one may be disadvantaged by their sex, origin, race, language, home, creed or religious and political beliefs.

Sex equality in appointments, pay and treatment at work is guaranteed through the basic law and by German ratification of ILO equality conventions. Federal Germany also amended its Civil Code in 1980 to incorporate the requirements of EC directives on equal treatment. Article 611 a of the Civil Code forbids discrimination against an employee in the sphere of appointments, except where a particular gender is an indispensable prerequisite for a particular job. The burden of proof rests with the employer to show that any discrimination shown to be taking place is justified on material grounds not related to the sex of the employee or by virtue of the necessity for the job to be done by someone of a particular gender.

Job descriptions or job advertisements may not specify a particular gender, unless it is justified on the grounds of necessity for the job.

Compensation for discrimination in appointments is based on a series of court rulings, guided by a decision of the European Court in a German case in 1984, which regard sex discrimination as a serious violation of individual rights under articles 823 and 847 of the Civil Code. Instead of awarding only out-of-pocket expenses incurred in the application, as before 1984, the courts will now award up to six months' salary in the post concerned if discrimination can be proved. The refusal of some courts to implement the European Court's principles until the domestic legislature had acted prompted the Federal government to bring forward legislation in spring 1990 which would provide for maximum compensation of four months' pay in the event of an applicant failing to be appointed on grounds of sex. Should discrimination take place during the recruitment process without this being the final reason for rejection of a female applicant, three months' pay in the post can be awarded. Where several applicants are discriminated against in the course of a single selection procedure the total amount of compensation payable to all may not exceed ten months' pay if several posts are open, or five months' in the event of one vacancy.

Disability. The 1986 Severely Disabled Persons Act requires all employers with at least sixteen posts to employ handicapped people—that is, people with at least a 50 per cent disability—in at least 6 per cent of those posts. Employers who fail to meet this quota are required to pay a sum of DM 150 per post. Employers are also obliged to see whether any vacancies could be filled by a severely handicapped person, and applications from the severely handicapped are to be discussed with the disabled employee's workplace representatives. Funds are available for adapting workplaces to the needs of the severely handicapped. The disability rating of employees is carried out by the occupational health section of the Federal Labour Office.

Employment incentives

The Federal Labour Office provides wage subsidies to employers for taking on:

- The unemployed in areas affected by high unemployment.
- Older or disabled workers.
- The long-term unemployed, irrespective of location, including money for training.

In the case of the long-term unemployed—who represent a growing proportion of those out of work—wage subsidies amount to up to 80 per cent of pay in the starting period, depending on how long the unemployed person has been without a job.

Offer and acceptance

Role of the works council

Works councils have rights of co-determination and consultation in two main areas specifically related to the commencement of employment in any establishment with more than twenty eligible employees. Firstly, works council approval is required for the use of any standard forms for contracts of employment. Secondly, the employer must inform the works council at least a week in advance of any proposed appointment, and provide details of the individual, their task and grade within the establishment, and all the application documents: these do not include the individual contract of employment or the results of any examination or test. There is a duty of confidentiality on works council members.

Exempted from this provision are board members or managing directors, and 'executives' (*leitende Angestellten*), defined as those who:

- Can engage or dismiss employees on their authority.
- Have power of attorney (*Prokura*) in major matters.
- Perform tasks which are important for the existence or development of the enterprise and which require particular experience or knowledge.
- Receive a salary which is either normal for executives in that enterprise, or regularly receive an annual salary which is three times the social security calculation base—around DM 118,400 (£40,136) in 1990.

However, the employer must inform the works council of the proposed appointment of such an executive. Where an Executive Representation Committee has been elected by managers, the employer must inform it of any proposed appointments.

The works council must respond within a week. It can object on any grounds it chooses, but the employer is legally bound initially to abide by the objection only if the appointment:

- Breaches a law, ordinance or safety regulation, collective or works agreement, court decision or official regulation.
- Breaches a guideline already agreed in the establishment.
- Might cause disadvantage to existing employees.

- Took place without an internal advertisement of the vacancy.
- Concerns a prospective employee who might disrupt 'industrial peace' in the establishment.

An employer may go to a labour court to reverse a works council objection. If the employer proceeds with the appointment in breach of the objection the employee may not begin actual employment but has a claim to be paid. Employers who ignore a court ruling can be obliged to give the employee notice, and to pay a fine of up to DM 500 (£170) per day of the employment.

There are procedures which allow employers to engage someone under urgent circumstances without informing the works council beforehand, but they must tell the council as soon as possible and explain why the appointment had to be dealt with urgently.

The form of the offer

There are no mandatory regulations which require a job offer or its acceptance to take a particular form, although collective agreements may specify that the contract of employment itself must follow an agreed format and/or be in writing. The law as it applies to the contract of employment as such is dealt with in a later volume of this series.

The basic law on the offer and acceptance of a contract is set out in the Civil Code, articles 147–57. An offer made direct to the applicant, either in person or by telephone, can be accepted immediately. An offer made by letter has to be responded to within a period of time which the employer would 'usually accept as reasonable'.

Should an employer delay too long in making a decision, and ultimately reject the applicant, he could be liable for damages and costs. The contract of employment itself follows from the acceptance, which could be demonstrated simply by the appointed applicant presenting himself or herself for work.

Work permits and papers

Citizens of EC member states, with the exception of Spain and Portugal, which are covered by transitional arrangements until the end of 1992, do not require a *work permit* (*Arbeitserlaubnis*) from the Labour Office in order to work in the Federal Republic. They will require a *residence permit* (*Aufenthaltserlaubnis*), which is normally granted as a formality for a period of five years. Individuals moving to Germany are required to register with the police.

Citizens of non-EC countries must apply for both a residence permit and a work permit. The residence permit has to be applied for before entry and takes the form of a visa in the holder's passport. Since the halt to the large-scale recruitment of overseas workers (the *Anwerbestopp*) in 1973 this is rarely granted, with some exceptions such as technical specialists.

No work permit is required for:

- Some categories of manager.
- Technicians sent by non-German firms for a period not exceeding two months.
- Academics.
- Students at German universities looking for work of no longer duration than two months a year.

Residence permits are usually issued to non-EC citizens for one year. The penalties for the illegal employment of non-EC residents can be severe.

Members of the families of foreign workers may apply for a work permit after a period of residence, depending on the economic circumstances of the sector in which they are looking for employment.

Work permits may be granted for a particular activity, for a particular undertaking, or for a particular district. Where the applicant is married to a German citizen, has asylum-seeker status and is legally resident in Germany, or has had a previous period of self-employment, the work permit will usually be issued without such restrictions.

The *work papers* which must be presented to a new employer for retention during employment comprise, apart from a work permit where appropriate:

- Tax card.
- Social insurance documents: from 1 July 1991 all employees will be required to have a social insurance pass, which

employees in certain industries, such as construction, must keep in their possession at work.
- Certificate indicating the amount of holiday taken, including educational release.
- Documentation of employee savings or share holdings for the purposes of employer capital formation payments under the state-supported employee savings scheme, if the employer is covered by a relevant collective agreement.

Employees will also have a statutory employment certificate (*Arbeitsbescheinigung*) from their previous employer, as well as a leaving certificate (*Zeugnis*), giving details of their employment record, which the new employer does not keep.

Should an applicant be rejected, all application documents must be returned. Any application form filled in by the applicant at the employer's request must be destroyed if the applicant so wishes, unless the employer has grounds—such as impending litigation—which warrant its retention.

Appendix

Organizations

Federal Ministry of Labour
(Bundesministerium für Arbeit und Sozialordnung):
5300 Bonn 1
Postfach 14 02 80
Rochustrasse 1
tel. +49 228 5271

Federal Employment Institute
(Bundesanstalt für Arbeit, BfA):
Regensburgerstrasse 104
8500 Nüremberg 30
tel. +49 911 170
fax +49 911 17 21 23
The Bundesanstalt currently operates regionally through nine state employment offices (*Landesarbeitsämter*) in each constituent state of the republic, and 150 local employment offices.
The Job, Servis and other temporary work agencies administered by the Bundesanstalt are represented in most large towns and cities.

Central Placement Office
(Zentralstelle für Arbeitsvermittlung, ZAV):
Feuerbachstrasse 42–46
6000 Frankfurt/Main 1
tel. +49 69 71110
fax +49 69 21 71 33 60

Recruitment in Germany

Federal Association of German
Management Consultants
(Bundesverband Deutscher
Unternehmensberater, BDU):
Friedrich-Wilhelm-Strasse 2
5300 Bonn 1
tel. +49 228 23 80 55
fax +49 228 23 06 25

Association of German
Personnel Consultants
(Arbeitskreis der
Personalberater in
Deutschland):
c/o Mülder & Co.
Frankfurt Airport Center
6000 Frankfurt 75

Federation for Temporary Work
(Bundesverband Zeitarbeit,
BZA):
Bachstrasse 1–3
5300 Bonn 1
tel. +49 228 63 24 50

British Chamber of Commerce
in Germany:
Heumarkt 14
5000 Cologne 1
tel. +49 221 234284

AUMA (Confederation of
German Trade Fair and
Exhibition Industries):
Lindenstrasse 8
5000 Cologne 1
tel. +49 221 209070
fax +49 221 2090712

Schutzgemeinschaft Zeitarbeit
e.V.
Hainer Weg 50
6000 Frankfurt/Main 70
tel. +49 69 61 80 68
fax +49 69 603 1287

AISEC e.V. (German branch)
Hohenzollernring 54
5000 Cologne 1
tel. +49 221 23 47 61

Confederation of German
Employers' Associations
(Bundesvereinigung der
deutschen Arbeitgeberverbände,
BDA):
Gustav Heinemann Ufer 72
5000 Cologne 51
tel. +49 221 37950
fax +49 221 37 95 235

German Personnel Management
Society (Deutsche Gesellschaft
für Personalführung, DGFP):
4000 Düsseldorf 1
Niederkasseler Lohweg 16
tel. +49 211 59 78 0
fax +49 211 59 78 505

German Trade Union
Confederation (Deutscher
Gewerkschaftsbund, DGB):
Hans-Böckler-Haus
Hans-Böckler-Strasse 39
4000 Düsseldorf 30
tel. +49 211 43011

Federal Vocational Training
Institute
(Bundesberufsbildungsinstitut):
Fehrbelliner Platz 3
1000 Berlin
tel. +49 30 8683280

Publications

Handelsblatt (Karriere):
Kasernenstrasse 67
4000 Düsseldorf
tel. +49 211 83 88 519
London office:
Thavies Inn House
3-4 Holborn Circus
London EC1N 2HB
tel. 071-353 3715

Frankfurter Allgemeine Zeitung (FAZ):
Hellerhofstrasse 2-4
6000 Frankfurt/Main
tel. +49 69 759 10
fax +49 69 759 1743

Süddeutsche Zeitung:
Sendlingerstrasse 80
Postfach 20 22 20
8000 Munich 8
tel. +49 89 2 18 30
fax +49 89 21 83787

Frankfurter Rundschau:
Postfach 10 06 60
Eschenheimer Strasse 16-18
6000 Frankfurt/Main
tel. +49 69 75 010
fax +49 69 21 99421

VDI-Nachrichten:
VDI Verlag GmbH
Postfach 8228
Heinrichstrasse 24
4000 Düsseldorf 1
tel. +49 211 61880
fax +49 211 6188112

Allgemeiner-Hochschul-Anzeiger:
as for *FAZ*

Forum (graduate recruitment magazine for university students: *Forum* also organizes recruitment fairs):
DSV Studenten Verlag GmbH
Bodanstrasse 2
9000 St Gallen
Switzerland
tel. +41 71 23 21 83

Karriereführer (contains information on graduate recruitment from *Fachhochschule*, together with 'green pages' listing companies recruiting graduates, including selection criteria and starting salaries):
Wison Verlag
Weyertal 59
5000 Cologne 41
tel. +49 221 44 30 31
fax +49 221 41 60 43

5
Recruitment in Greece

Recruiting executives and specialists is likely to get harder, and more expensive, in the early 1990s. Companies seeking to establish themselves in Greece will be competing for talent with local firms looking to add marketing and personnel skills to their operations against the background of the single market. Although there is no generalized shortage of school leavers, there are shortages, in some cases severe, of qualified and motivated graduates. Skilled blue-collar workers are also in short supply, especially in provincial labour markets outside the Athens area, and the shortfalls in training encourage poaching. However, companies positioning themselves in the upper levels of the market—either through higher pay, career development or reputation—can find a pool of potential executive talent, often highly educated to second-degree level at US or British universities and with excellent language skills.

Local practitioners point to the following problem areas in recruitment:

- Low level of employee mobility.
- Dismissal provisions may deter large-scale hiring.
- Shortages of finance and accountancy personnel.
- Care needed in integrating new managers into existing structures, especially if the status of current employees is affected.

To quote one senior Greek personnel manager with a multinational employer, 'Recruitment is not problematic, but it needs proper attention.'

The labour market

The working population in 1987 stood at 4,069,000 out of a total population of some 10 million. Total employment was 3,780,000, although of this total only just over half were employees, with the bulk of the remainder accounted for by family workers or the armed forces. This ratio of employees to the whole work force, at 52 per cent, is one of the lowest in Europe, and compares with 88 per cent in the UK and 70 per cent in Spain. A quarter of the working population still work in agriculture.

Most workers, including those in industry, work in very small enterprises. Public-sector employment is also high. The number of workers with the skills and background suited to employment in a non-Greek company is relatively small compared with the total — and overwhelmingly concentrated in the Athens area.

The population of working age grew slightly faster than the OECD European average during the 1980s, but fell behind much of Europe as the decade drew to a close. A modest but steady rise in the total participation rate, however, enabled the total labour force to keep growing ahead of the European average in the late 1980s. Labour force participation, although lower than in northern Europe, is above most other regions in EC member states in the Mediterranean. Much of the increased participation has come from a substantial expansion in the number of women entering employment. Women's participation in the labour force rose from 33 per cent to 43 per cent between 1979 and 1988, putting it on a par with Italy, compared with a fall for men from 79 per cent to 75 per cent.

The labour force is expected to grow by 0·7 per cent in 1991, almost a halving of the pace of the mid-1980s, but on a par with Spain and Italy and above most countries in northern Europe. Officially registered unemployment is running at around 8 per cent, equivalent to 300,000 people.

There are estimated to be around 130,000 foreign workers, about 3 per cent of the work force, the majority from the Third World, but only an estimated 32,000 have work permits. Many are engaged in domestic service, or carry out routine manual work — especially in the provinces.

After peaking in the mid-1980s, growth in the 15–24 year old age group is set to slow down during the 1990s. The 15–44 age group is expected to increase only very slightly by the year 2000, with a fall in the 45–64 year age group over this period.

The freeze in public-sector jobs, and possible contraction of the public sector, could release experienced employees on to the labour market, easing certain skill shortages and encouraging young people to look beyond the state as an employer. Ironically, in view of skill shortages in many specialisms, unemployment among the most educationally qualified remains high—at around 30 per cent—reflecting, as the OECD comments, 'aspirations to find permanent and well paid jobs in the public sector'.

Personnel planning

Official notification

The Greek constitution provides for both freedom of occupation and the employer's freedom to hire. Companies making use of EC employment subsidies are required to take 50 per cent of new hirings from employees sent to them by the Labour Administration (OAED), which runs both vocational training and the state job placement system.

All new hirings have to be notified to OAED within eight days of the appointment. Failure to do so will not invalidate the appointment but does make the employer liable to a fine. (This is a relaxation of the statutory requirement for all hiring to be carried out via OAED.) Notification must also be made to IKA, the state social insurance fund, and there are penalties in the form of supplementary contributions for failure to do so.

All dismissals must be notified to OAED.

Companies are required to submit three-monthly returns to the labour authorities on employee numbers and six-monthly information on hours and pay to the Labour Inspectorate.

There are no statutory or agreed requirements on consultation with the work force on personnel planning or proposed hiring.

Using part-timers and temps

Both part-time and fixed-term contracts are permissible. In the past the use of *part-timers* has been complicated by legal regulations on social security. In order to obtain the minimum legally required social security coverage, employees had to work for at least four hours a day, setting a floor for employers of twenty hours a week, irrespective of their needs. Part-time work is still 'atypical' in Greece, with only 4 per cent of total employees working on this basis, compared with just over 10 per cent in

France, Belgium and Germany, and nearly a quarter in the UK: 8 per cent of Greek female employees work part-time compared with 44 per cent in the UK.

Legislation before parliament in the summer of 1990, intended to liberalize working hours and reform redundancy provisions in ailing industries, will provide for a new social insurance category for part-timers enabling fewer than four hours a day to be worked.

Fixed-term contracts are widely used in agriculture and tourism, and also by consumer-goods companies for seasonal products and sales campaigns. Companies are free to arrange such contracts direct with the temporary employee but must specify the duration of the agreement and the hours to be worked. Care should be taken in renewing fixed-term contracts. A fixed-term contract may be renewed once, but any further renewals could lead to the employment relationship being deemed permanent by the courts if the gap between contracts is insufficient. Companies who use temporary staff often have alternating teams of workers on fixed-term contracts.

Agency staff can be obtained by companies needing short-term secretarial help. As with cleaning and security staff—other typical agency-provided workers—these remain employees of the agency and are provided as part of an overall service by firms which advertise as providers of office or industrial services. A number of established firms, some of which are subsidiaries of major international providers of temporary employees, operate on this basis and are used by reputable international employers.

Employment agencies also exist to provide workers for permanent placement with an employer. As Greece has ratified ILO Conventions 88 and 96, which provide for the abolition of fee-charging employment agencies, these have no legal standing as such. However, a distinction should be drawn between the accepted practice of executive and professional search, which we deal with below, and the provision of workers by agencies who take a cash commission and supply staff who are also paid 'off the books'. (The 'black economy' is estimated to be worth around an additional 30 per cent of reported gross domestic product.)

Established companies with a permanent and unionized work

force could experience problems in moving to more 'flexible' arrangements or introducing contractors.

Finding the applicant

Very different methods apply, depending on whether an organization is looking for managers and specialists or blue-collar and routine white-collar staff. We turn first to blue- and routine white-collar employees.

The state placement system

The state placement system, OAED, is used by some companies to obtain blue-collar workers, generally unskilled, but suffers from a generally poor reputation, with companies reporting that its results were often disappointing and the service inefficient. Because most people on OAED's books are the registered unemployed, many school leavers who could find jobs through the service are not available for placement. Moreover, only about one-eighth of the unemployed actually register with the service — the lowest rate in the European Community.

Nonetheless, companies looking for particular blue-collar or technical skills have found OAED useful as part of a broader recruitment campaign because of its coverage and search capacity. It is more widely used in the provinces than in Athens. Efforts are in hand to improve OAED's services and raise its usefulness to employers.

All new hirings must be notified to OAED within eight days.

A recent survey carried out among 2,000 workers by the central trade union organization, the Federation of Greek Workers, found that only 3 per cent had found their current job via OAED, compared with 60 per cent who found work through a personal introduction, friend or acquaintance, and 14 per cent through an agency.

These findings confirm company reports. By and large, only rarely do established companies advertise blue-collar or routine vacancies or use the state system, tending instead to rely on the spread of knowledge about vacancies through informal family, friendship, neighbourhood and trade union channels. Those that do advertise vacancies seldom mention their company name when looking for blue-collar workers, unless there is a particular policy of developing the firm's image as an employer. (Companies which did cite their name were vehement about doing so positively to attract top-class applicants.) In general, there was concern that using the firm's name was likely to be followed by a constant telephone bombardment of the personnel manager by applicants. Job advertisements are therefore usually placed under an agent's or consultant's name, or use a box number.

Good employers—especially foreign-owned companies which tend to pay at the top end of the pay range—rely heavily on internal development and training for obtaining skilled blue-collar workers, such as maintenance engineers, and build on the skills acquired through the state vocational training system. There is often strong internal pressure for vacancies involving promotion to be filled from existing employees. Nevertheless, because of skill shortages and the mismatch between the education and training system and job requirements, poaching for specialist staff is common.

Because of compulsory military service, a skilled engineering worker trained in a state-run vocational school and looking for his first job will be at least 23 years old.

There are more informal ways in which employers and employees can get together. In the building industry, for example, workers regularly gather in Omonia Square, one of the main squares in Athens; and ship repair workers congregate outside the municipal buildings. Caritas, a charity, tries to find short-term employment for foreign workers.

Finding professional and executive staff

External recruitment to fill a professional vacancy, ranging from executive secretary to CEO, either via advertising or consultants, accounted for a third of appointments in 1988: two-thirds of vacancies were filled by internal promotion or personal reference.

In an analysis of advertised demand in 1988 carried out by consultants Stedima, some 30 per cent of foreign-owned companies looking for professional and managerial staff used consultants, compared with 70 per cent who advertised directly in the press under their own name. (Around double the percentage of foreign companies used consultants compared with local firms.) The proportion going to consultants is a good deal higher for executive positions and among newly established foreign firms. Greek-owned firms still tend to use consultants simply to find, rather than select, candidates, and then frequently only as a last resort.

Consultants may be used simply as a means of advertising anonymously, may carry out some pre-selection, or may undertake full-scale executive search activities. Organizations established to recruit and place staff have no legal standing as such, but function as advisers to firms on appointments within the context of business consultancy and are subject to company law provisions which govern service organizations.

There is no professional organization of executive search consultants (a formal association would require twenty members) and the half-dozen or so main players of high standing are essentially self-regulating within a framework of mutual competition and commercial common sense. Consultants may not approach a client's employees and would not handle an application from such an employee in response to an anonymous advertisement. The consensus among practitioners is that consultants could handle former placements after a lapse of five years.

There are two customary methods of charging fees. Either the search consultancy receives a fee, typically around 15 per cent of the first year's total cash remuneration of the employee, plus the cost of advertising, or an all-in fee of 18 per cent, with the consultancy free to choose whether, how and where to advertise the position. A third of the fee is usually paid in advance, with a third on presentation of a short list and a further third on selection.

The market for professional employees tightened in the late 1980s: although there has been a trough in reported demand of 14 per cent between 1989 and 1990, the supply side of the professional market—measured by the reported response of a sample of companies—fell by nearly 50 per cent. According to Stedima, who carried out the survey, one explanation could lie in an upward shift in pay and bonuses in the wake of higher corporate profits, leading to a slowdown in the rate of staff turnover.

Shortages of financially qualified personnel have become severe, reflected in the fact that the most frequent resort to recruitment consultants has been to find cost accountants, business analysts and finance directors. Along with personnel executives, accountants and financial executives were the only sectors which saw any growth in reported demand between the first quarters of 1989 and 1990, but their mobility is testified to by the fact that they continued to respond to advertisements, where other functions held back.

Skilled personnel managers were also reported by companies to be in high demand, reflecting the need to establish more effective recruitment and internal development against a background of a tighter market for skilled staff and the need to retain employees. The personnel function is still comparatively undeveloped but is recognized as an area of growing importance.

Marketing skills, developed most comprehensively among multinational companies in Greece, are also in demand by local firms, and demand for marketing positions has broadly held up against the generally slackening trend in new executive demand during 1989/90.

Graduates

The limited supply of higher education places, compared with strong demand from qualified school leavers, has led to between a quarter and a third of all Greek students undertaking university education abroad, with the USA and the UK still strongly favoured for both first and especially for second degrees. Most come back, creating a pool of qualified graduates with excellent English and experience of organizational, and possibly business, life outside Greece.

Companies recruiting graduates for management development tend to look for two degrees, with some preference for a first degree from a Greek higher education establishment and a second degree obtained abroad. Some foreign universities run first and second-year degree courses in Greece, giving credits to those who move on to a final degree at their home campus. A degree outside Greece is especially looked for in the natural sciences and for those entering sales and marketing. Foreign-owned companies also recruit MBAs, and in some cases these account for 30 per cent or even more, of the graduate intake. Whereas foreign-owned companies operating in Greece tend to look for qualifications as a sign that the individual has potential for development, Greek companies—particularly smaller, family-owned concerns—opt for experience. Graduates in accountancy and finance need a Greek degree and qualification and must be a member of the local professional organization. The business schools of Athens, Piraeus and Salonika are highly regarded.

The prime demand for graduates is for those with business and finance qualifications, followed by engineering and computing.

Greek universities are only beginning to develop careers advice and recruitment organizations. The American College of Greece (details in the appendix) holds an annual graduate recruitment fair, and students at the School of Business at Piraeus University who are members of AIESEC organize their own recruitment event. Companies therefore tend to develop their own contacts with universities and private colleges and their teaching staff, as do the principal recruitment consultants.

Newspaper advertising is used to find graduates, and firms also receive many unsolicited C.V.s.

There is no particular hiring season for graduates, largely because the obligation for men to do military service after graduation evens out the flow of graduates on to the labour market. Military service currently varies from twenty to twenty-four months, depending on the branch of the military involved, but is expected to be reduced in the future to fifteen to eighteen months. Women do not have to do military service. On average, a male graduate with a first degree looking for his first job will be at least 25–26 years of age, or 27–28 in the case of graduates with a second degree.

Starting salaries for a graduate with no work experience in mid-1990 ranged from Dr 80,000 per month for a graduate with a first degree to Dr 130,000 per month for a second-degree holder, probably from a foreign university or a top-flight Greek college. Salaries are paid fourteen times a year, giving a range of Dr 1,120,000–1,820,000 (£4,100–£6,600).

Advertising media

We have already touched on the subject of advertising. To recapitulate, advertising is widely used for recruiting managers and specialists, either directly under the company's name or via a consultant. Advertising is less used for blue-collar workers, and companies need to consider whether they want to advertise under their own name or use a consultant, media agency or box number to collect applications. The British-Hellenic Chamber of

Commerce in Athens can provide information and guidance on organizations and the services available.

The main vehicle for job advertisements across all categories is the national daily newspaper *Ta Nea*, which carries advertisements on most days, with a job column on Wednesdays. The professional engineers' organization TEE (Technical Chamber of Greece) has a fortnightly journal, *Technika Chronica*, which some companies use for locating technical specialists. The business and financial daily *Express* is used for some white-collar advertising, especially in finance, as is the daily paper *Naftemboriki* and *To Vima*. In general, the specialist press is not highly developed as a vehicle for job advertisements.

Jobs can be advertised in either Greek or English, and there are no legal constraints on setting age limits. English-language advertisements are frequently used as a means of pre-selection for jobs requiring it as a prerequisite. Salary ranges are only very rarely stated in job advertisements.

Selection

In contrast to much of the European Community, there is very largely a legal vacuum in the area of selection methods. A general obligation to maintain confidentiality exists, and is enforceable in civil law. Draft legislation on data protection exists, but has so far made little progress. There is no code of practice issued by an employer or personnel organization.

Recruitment consultants may include confidentiality clauses in contracts and candidate submission reports, and will endeavour to control client access to information about the applicant.

Although it is difficult to quantify, the culture of recruitment and employment does seem to sanction a greater degree of inquisitiveness about personal circumstances than in the UK. Certainly a manager would expect to be asked about family background and origins, and a woman about her marriage and family plans—questions which would be technically illegal and to which candidates could exercise a 'right to lie' elsewhere in the Community. In law, a woman may not be asked whether she is pregnant, and is protected against dismissal if she is. As anywhere else, politics should be avoided and sensibilities may be acute.

Interviewing is the prime method of selection, and candidates looking for employment in a foreign-owned company or for a senior position would expect at least two or three interviews for graduate appointees, and four, five or six for senior managers. Psychometric tests and graphology are rarely, if ever, used by companies—none was reported as part of this study. Consultants, however, would tend to use psychometric testing for senior managers. Aptitude tests would be used for technical and secretarial positions, and in some cases firms might also use IQ tests.

Companies will ask for a medical examination, degree certificates and details of any criminal offences. Medical examinations will be normally carried out by a doctor appointed by the company, and in general the physician will report only on whether the candidate is fit for employment or not, a full report of the results going only to the applicant.

Appointees need to obtain a statement of their criminal record from the legal authorities. Less serious offences drop out of the record after a predetermined period.

It is usual to take up references. Three references are customary, but company practice differs on the value of talking to the candidate's current employer.

Offers and rejections

The form of the offer

There are no legal requirements on making offers or rejecting applicants. Applications from candidates for posts advertised by recruiters would invariably be acknowledged in writing, and most job advertisements would contain a statement to that effect.

A written offer is a rarity, except when the job is for a fixed-term, as under Greek law an employment contract of indefinite duration is an oral agreement.

In a survey of hirings effected via a recruitment consultancy, the average length of time needed for a recruitment decision after receipt of a list of proposed candidates from the recruiter was fifty days, with Greek companies taking fifty-six days and foreign companies needing forty-five. (The recruiter's own activity consumed about two months.)

Work permits

Since 1988 there has been free movement of labour between Greece and the rest of the European Community, with the exception of Spain and Portugal.

Foreign nationals need to apply for a work permit to the Ministry of Labour, although technical staff in industrial and mining organizations may be employed before the permit has been received, provided the Labour Inspectorate is notified.

Appendix

Organizations

OAED (the state manpower and job placement agency):
Thrakis 8
166.10 Glyfada
Athens
tel. +30 1 993 2589
fax +30 1 993 7301

Ministry of Labour:
40 Piraeus Street
Athens
tel. +30 1 523 3110

Federation of Greek Industries (represents employers in manufacturing and services, and negotiates general collective agreements with the Confederation of Labour, the central trade union organization):
5 Xenofentos Street
105 57 Athens
tel. +30 1 323 7325
The federation also has regional offices.

Greek Personnel Management Association (personnel managers in companies with at least fifty employees with a distinct personnel function may join; the association produces salary and benefit surveys and seeks to exercise influence on employment matters):
3 Karitsi Street
G-105 61 Athens
tel. +30 1 322 5704

British–Hellenic Chamber of Commerce:
25 Vas. Sofias
106 74 Athens
tel. +30 1 721 0361
fax +30 1 721 8571

Stedima SA, business consultants:
29 Michalakopoulou
115 28 Athens
tel. +30 1 724 5541
fax +30 1 724 9508

American College of Greece
(Deree College holds an annual recruitment fair):
contact:
The Career Counsellor
6 Gravias
153 42 Paraskevi
tel. +30 1 639 3250

Publications

Ta Nea ('The News'):
3 Christou Lada Street
102 376 Athens
tel. +30 1 32 50 611
fax +30 1 32 28 797

Express:
Halandriou Road
Amaroussion
Athens
tel. +30 1 68 27 582

To Vima:
(as for Ta Nea)

Acknowledgements

The authors are indebted to Stedima SA, business consultants, for their contribution to this section.

6
Recruitment in the Irish Republic

The labour market is characterized by persistently high unemployment paralleled by high levels of emigration of skilled and specialist staff to the US and Europe, particularly the UK. It is increasingly difficult for locally based employers to fill specialist and managerial posts. Although the number of graduates produced in Ireland is relatively small, they represent an attractive pool of skilled labour to UK employers, having the advantages of a common language and similar educational background. Graduate recruitment to elsewhere in Europe is, as yet, minor in scale. Local companies looking to attract highly qualified managerial and specialist staff are seeking alternatives to offering high pay, which is heavily taxed compared with the UK.

Although Ireland has a high birth rate and high unemployment, recent economic growth has resulted in skill shortages for blue- and white-collar workers in a number of areas which have experienced strong growth recently, such as computing. Skill shortages are forecast to remain high in certain sectors, such as IT, construction, health care, marketing and financial services.

School leavers are also in increasingly short supply, as a growing number of young people of school leaving age are choosing to go on to higher education.

Local practitioners list the following areas as the most problematic when recruiting new staff:

- Shortage of school leavers.
- Lack of graduates with appropriate skills.
- Shortages of managers and professionals.

The labour market

The labour force amounted to 1,310,000 persons in 1988, representing an overall participation rate of approximately 60 per cent of those of working age, among the lowest in the European Community. And although, according to OECD figures, male participation was well up amongst Community member states, the female rate, at 37 per cent, was the lowest. In contrast to other Community countries with similar low female participation in paid work, the Irish Republic has seen only a very modest rise of 3 per cent in this figure since the early 1970s.

Part-time work, as measured by Eurostat, accounted for only 7·6 per cent of employees in 1987, with women making up around 75 per cent of part-time workers.

The work force is becoming more qualified, with a shrinking proportion of people leaving school early and a growing number going on to gain tertiary qualifications. Between 1981 and 1986 the proportion of young people in full-time education in the 15–19 year old group rose from 54 per cent to 60 per cent, and in the 20–24 year old group from 7 per cent to nearly 10 per cent. The number of persons holding a technological or scientific qualification at degree level had also increased, from 35,500 in 1981 to just over 50,000 by the mid-1980s.

Although Ireland has not suffered demographic change to the same degree as the UK and some other European countries, companies still cite a shortage of young qualified staff as one of their main recruitment problems. Emigration, mainly to the US and the UK, continues to draw away skilled workers and specialists: 46,000 people migrated in the year to April 1989, compared with 32,000 the preceding year. The proportion of graduates finding work abroad rose from 5 per cent in 1982 to 19·9 per cent in 1988. Since the actual number of graduates finding work at home has remained stable during that time, the temptation of overseas employment has soaked up the steady increase in the number of graduates from higher education institutions achieved in recent years.

From being a problem in the early 1980s, graduate unemployment has fallen, from 11 per cent in 1982 to 3·9 per cent, with skill shortages in sectors such as engineering, financial services and computing. However, graduate emigration continues to rise, from 14·3 per cent in 1984 to 26·1 per cent in 1988. The UK labour market accounts for around 70 per cent, with 10 per cent going to the US, and around 1 per cent to continental Europe — a figure likely to increase, however, as European companies become increasingly anxious to recruit well educated Irish graduates.

Personnel planning

Work-force consultation

Companies are not legally obliged to consult trade unions or employee representatives on personnel planning issues, but larger companies tend to have in-house arrangements, some companies having union agreements which stipulate that all internal vacancies must be posted up. With this type of agreement, employees usually have a time limit in which to apply. The employer usually reserves the right to recruit externally if no suitable applicants have been found within the company.

Using part-timers and temps

Temporary work. There are very few legal constraints on temporary employment agencies, which operate in the same way as in the UK, with many chains familiar in the UK also operating in the Republic. Workers employed by companies on a temporary contract tend to be employed for less than twelve months, as any temporary staff with more than one year's service are entitled to the rights of permanent employees, such as periods of notice and sick and holiday pay.

There are no specific definitions or regulations on *part-time work*. Employees must work a minimum of eighteen hours a week, and have three years' continuous service, to qualify for minimum periods of notice in the event of dismissal.

There are no statutory quotas for the employment of *disabled workers* in the private sector. In the civil service and public-sector a target of 3 per cent of the work force was set in 1981, although according to the National Rehabilitation Board the number of disabled workers in any one organization has never accounted for more than 1·4 per cent of the work force.

Finding the applicant

Employers can recruit staff directly, by advertisement or individual approach, through the state job placement agency, FAS, or through private employment agencies for both temporary and permanent placement. Advertising was the main medium for reaching sales, marketing and managerial staff, and agencies accounted for around a quarter of the sample, with greater agency involvement in the accountancy and financial services sphere, according to a study carried out by Atlas Personnel Services Group, which looked at how 300 surveyed individuals found their present position. Around 30 per cent of vacancies were filled by word of mouth or speculative application.

Private agencies are governed by the Employment Equality Act, which stipulates that an employment agency must not discriminate:

- In the terms on which it offers to provide any of its services.
- By refusing or omitting to provide any of its services.
- In the manner in which it provides any of its services.

These provisions do not apply where the service only concerns employment which an employer could lawfully refuse to offer to the person concerned (Employment Equality Act, section 7(3)).

An employment agency will not be held liable for discrimination if it can prove that it acted in accordance with statements made by the employer, that its actions would not be unlawful under section 7(3) above, and if it can prove that it was reasonable for it to rely on the statements.

Employers who knowingly make false statements in order to obtain services from an agency are liable to a fine of up to Ir£200 (£185).

The official placement system

The state job placement and training agency (FAS) plays an active role in job placement and mediation between employers and job seekers as well as in the development of training programmes. A total of 14,675 vacancies were filled and 24,122 vacant posts were advertised through the FAS in 1989. The agency also offers information services to all job seekers covering areas such as careers advice and advice on working abroad. It also offers a number of training courses to the unemployed.

FAS services to employers include the pre-selection and aptitude testing of candidates, and various incentive schemes designed to encourage employers to take on the long-term unemployed and disadvantaged early school leavers.

Recruitment agencies and consultants

The professional body representing management consulting firms is the Association of Management Consulting Organizations (AMCO). It lists its aims as:

- Promoting a wider understanding and use of consultancy services in industry, commerce and government.
- Encouraging high standards of professional service among member firms.
- Contributing to discussions at national level concerning the industrial and commercial life of the country.
- International representation of Irish management consultancy through membership of FEACO, the European Federation of Consulting Organizations.

AMCO member firms offer services across the whole consulting range, including personnel and industrial relations, training, the behavioural sciences, remuneration policies and systems, management sciences, and organization studies. AMCO has issued a code of practice for its members, who have adopted it voluntarily. The main points include:

Candidate care and confidentiality. Identifiable details about a candidate or potential candidate will be revealed to a client and enquiries regarding a candidates references will be dealt with only with the specific knowledge and consent of the candidate. Candidates always have the right to know the client's identity before the consultants disclose their identity to the client. Information given by the client or by candidates in confidence will be kept confidential and may be used only in connection with a recruitment assignment. All candidates will be kept informed of the progress of their application, and unsuccessful candidates will be advised when an appointment is made or the assignment is otherwise completed. On completion of an assignment, upon request, the consultants will destroy an unsuccessful candidate's file. Consultants will provide candidates, upon written request, free of charge, with a copy of their personal history form if it is held on their files. In no circumstances will a candidate be charged a fee.

Client relations. The consultant can accept a recruitment assignment only when the client provides adequate information for analysing the situation to which candidate qualifications are to be matched; clients may be required to produce references. A consultant will not knowingly accept a recruitment assignment on which another consultant is already engaged. The fee basis must be agreed with the client beforehand. If an advertising campaign does not produce a suitable candidate for employment or if the selected candidate does not accept an appointment the consultants will continue to work on the assignment on the fee basis originally agreed until it is completed or abandoned. Consultants will not solicit a job application from persons placed with their present employer through their recruitment service. Consultants are responsible for ensuring that candidates are informed of progress by the consultant or, at short-list stage by the client.

A full copy of the code of practice can be obtained from AMCO (see appendix).

Advertising

Advertising relating to employment is governed by the Employment Equality Act, 1977, which prohibits discrimination, direct or indirect, on grounds of sex or marital status with regard to access to employment and promotion, access to vocational training and work experience, and conditions of employment. The Act is currently being reviewed in the Department of Labour. A paper setting out the Labour Minister's intentions or draft legislation to amend the Act and the Anti-Discrimination (Pay) Act, 1974, is expected during the course of 1990/91.

Section 8 of the Employment Equality Act stipulates that it is unlawful to classify a post by reference to sex except where the sex of the person is an occupational qualification for the post. An employer who makes a false statement in order to secure publication or display of a discriminatory advertisement is liable to a fine not exceeding Ir£200 (£185). This would be the case if, for example, an employer persuaded an agency to display a job advertisement by assuring it that the job was open to either sex when the real intention was to employ one sex only. Even if, in practice, only one sex is likely to be qualified for a particular job, advertisements cannot lawfully imply that an employer is seeking applications from one sex only.

Indirect discrimination is a less clear-cut area; the Labour Court has found that the following can also be discriminatory:

- The imposition of maximum age limits.
- The setting of minimum height requirements.
- A requirement that applicants should be prepared to be mobile throughout the country.

The Employment Equality Agency recommends that recruitment by word of mouth should be avoided on the grounds of possible implications for indirect discrimination: 'recruitment solely or primarily by word of mouth in a work force of predominantly one sex should be avoided'. No relevant case has occurred so far, but eyes have been cast at instances raised under the UK Race Relations Act, where it was held that, if a work force were predominantly of one race in a department where the vacancy arose, staff might recommend another person of their own race.

Many companies use newspaper advertisements to attract white-collar and managerial staff. According to a survey carried out by the recruitment agency Executive Market, a total of 5,643 jobs were advertised in the national press in the year to April 1990. Advertising for professional and scientific services accounted for 24 per cent of job adverts, with electronics representing 15·4 per cent and commerce 13·9 per cent. Sales account for the greatest number of vacancies with 19·1 per cent of all jobs advertised, followed by accountants, with 12·2 per cent. Most of the jobs advertised were at professional level (52 per cent), with 38 per cent of adverts requiring junior staff.

The *Irish Times* carried around 50 per cent of all the vacancies surveyed, and 57 per cent of all professional and middle-management advertisements, with a pull-out labour market and recruitment section every Friday. Other newspapers which carry advertisements are the *Sunday Independent*, the *Irish Indepen-*

dent, the *Sunday Tribune*, the *Sunday Press* and the *Sunday Business Post*.

Only fifty advertisements were recorded for senior jobs involving either the management of a company with a turnover of Ir£500 million (£460 million) or of 300 employees, someone reporting direct to them, or a chief executive for a smaller firm. The survey is available from Executive Market (see appendix).

The specialist UK press is also used for specific occupations.

Companies placing advertisements for staff in newspapers generally use their company name but tend on the whole not to give salary details.

Graduate recruitment

There are careers services both at the constituent colleges of the National University of Ireland (University College Dublin, University College Cork and University College Galway), as well as Trinity College Dublin. All are members of the UK Association of Graduate Careers Advisory Services. The services provide both counselling and placement, including advice to potential employers.

There is no military service. First-degree courses normally require three years in the arts and social sciences, and four years in technical and scientific disciplines.

Application documents

There is no official obligation to consult trades unions or employee representatives on the content of application documents, nor is there any specific legislation concerning what can and cannot be asked on application forms. However, on the basis of a number of cases of discrimination taken to the Equal Opportunities Court, the Equal Opportunities Agency has issued a number of recommendations regarding application documents:

- Employers should ensure that all persons who handle job applications in any form or capacity, or give information on job vacancies, do not state or imply that members of one sex or a particular marital status will be favoured for a job.
- Application forms should be simple and clear, and should

not require unnecessary or irrelevant information, particularly concerning personal circumstances. Recourse to questions relating to family status should be avoided on application forms and in the conduct of interviews, as they may be taken as evidence of an intention to discriminate.
- Where selection tests are carried out, they should relate directly to the actual requirements of the job. The content of such tests should not include matters likely to favour persons of one sex above another.

Under the 1987 Data Protection Act employees are entitled to request written extracts of data kept on computer concerning them, and to have incorrect information rectified.

Selection

Interviews still constitute the main method of selection. Under the Employment Equality Act, it is unlawful to discriminate on the grounds of sex or marital status, and employees who feel they have been discriminated against may take their case to an Equal Opportunities or Labour Court.

The Equal Opportunities Agency's code of practice includes guidelines on interviews:

- Where possible, interview boards should not be comprised of persons of one sex only, and all persons who conduct or participate in interviews should always be carefully trained in the avoidance of discrimination.
- Where practicable, records of interviews should be kept, showing clearly why applicants were or were not selected.
- Questions should refer to the requirements of the job. Care should be taken that questions relating to marriage plans, family planning intentions, children, etc., should not be asked where they could be construed as indicating bias against women. Where it is necessary to assess whether personal circumstances will affect the performance of the job (such as where the job involves unsocial hours or extensive travel) relevant questions, where they are deemed absolutely necessary, should be asked equally of male and female applicants,

and the answers should be evaluated on the same basis for each.
- In all cases an interviewer should explain why a particular question is being asked if its relevance may not be immediately obvious.

Penalties imposed on employers for discrimination can range from Ir£400 (£365) to Ir£12,000 (£11,000).

Job simulation and aptitude tests are a frequent part of the selection process. The Employment Equality Agency recommends that when selection tests are carried out they should relate directly to the actual requirements of the job. The content of such tests should not include matters likely to favour persons of one sex above another.

References. There is no legal obligation for employers to provide a former employee with any reference or testimonial, although they are frequently asked to provide reference documents concerning an employee or former employee. The person requesting the references must have the consent of the employee. If a reference is proved false in any way, the provider is in contravention of the law on three possible accounts: defamation, which consists of making a false statement that harms the reputation of another; negligent misstatement, in which an employer may be liable for loss or damages suffered by a former employee following misinformation in a reference; or deceit, in which it must be proved that a false statement was made deliberately with the intention that it should be acted upon.

According to a survey of reference-checking practices in 146 companies in the manufacturing, service and public sectors, reported in the Dublin-based journal *Industrial Relations News*, 90 per cent of the companies collected references at some stage in the selection process; 88 per cent did so after the interview. Fifty per cent of these companies said that they would request permission from the candidate before requesting references. Sixty-four per cent of the companies said that they would check some of the reference information, mainly educational record, previous employment record, credit and police records. The three main types of reference commonly used are character, school and employer references.

Criminal record. Questions or check-ups on previous criminal records are not generally deemed to be relevant to a job application. However, an employer may ask about absence records and check them with the previous employer.

Offer and rejection

There is no legal regulation of the form for making a job offer or receiving confirmation of acceptance. However, in practice job offers and acceptances tend to be written, mainly to ensure that a record is kept of all transactions. A letter offering employment may contain terms of employment, such as rates of pay, working hours, holiday entitlement, probationary periods, pension schemes and notice periods.

Rejection of applicants

There is no specific legislation relating to the rejection of applicants. In practice unsuitable candidates are sent a letter of rejection. They may contact companies to ask why they were not successful. Companies are under no obligation to disclose the information unless the case is taken to court because of, for example, discrimination charges.

Work permits

Work permits are not required by EC nationals but all other foreign workers must apply to the Department of Labour for a work permit before commencing employment. Work permits are issued for a maximum period of one year and are renewable.

Appendix

Organizations

Department of Labour:
Mespil Road
Dublin 4
tel. (01) 765861

Training and Employment
Authority (FAS):
27 Upper Baggot Street
Dublin 4
tel. (01) 685777
fax (01) 682691

Federation of Irish Employers
(FIE):
Baggot Bridge House
84–6 Lower Baggot Street
Dublin 2
tel. (01) 601011
fax (01) 601717

Irish Congress of Trade Unions
(ICTU):
19 Raglan Road
Dublin 4
tel. (01) 680641
fax (01) 609027

Association of Management
Consulting Organizations
(AMCO):
Confederation House
Kildare Street
Dublin 2
tel. (01) 779801

Irish IPM:
35–9 Shelbourne Road
Ballsbridge
Dublin 4
tel. (01) 686244

National University of Ireland:
University College Dublin
Administration Building
Belfield
Dublin 4
tel. (01) 693244

University College Cork
Cork City
tel. (021) 276871

University College Galway
Galway City
tel. (091) 24411

Trinity College Dublin:
College Green
Dublin 2
tel. (01) 772941

Executive Market:
Bay House
120 Rock Road
Booterstown
Co. Dublin
tel. (01) 834474
fax (01) 834472

Publication

The Irish Times:
P.O. box 74
11–15 D'Olier Street
Dublin 2
tel. (01) 6792022
fax (01) 6793910

7
Recruitment in Italy

Recruitment in Italy can be both practically and administratively difficult, and, because of skill shortages, also an expensive process. Local practitioners expect recruitment to get more difficult in the future. Companies therefore have an incentive to minimize turnover and find candidates for promotion internally.

The labour market is characterized by a number of features which can make recruitment, especially of manual and routine white-collar workers, more circuitous than is the norm in the United Kingdom. 'Atypical work' is also atypical, with little part-time work, and legal obstacles to temporary employment. Aspects to note include:

- The need for an intimate understanding of how the bureaucracy functions and the emphasis on personal contacts.
- The low level of regional mobility and strength of local ties.
- The lack of graduates with appropriate qualifications.

The labour market

In 1989 the labour force totalled 23,870,000 workers, of which some 2,865,000 were unemployed, an unemployment rate of 12 per cent, amongst the highest in the European Community. Important regional and demographic imbalances lurk behind the bald figures, however. While unemployment in northern and central Italy has fallen since 1985, it has continued to grow in the south. For example, while there is virtually no male unemployment in the 25–59 year age group in the north and centre, the southern unemployment rate for this group was running at around 8 per cent in the late 1980s. This regional disparity is even more pronounced among women and young people. Since industry agreements are negotiated nationally and centrally, and labour mobility is low, wage pressure acting on minimum rates in the north can raise pay in the south and is held to be one reason why unemployment has been so intractable there.

In 1989 the OECD estimated that some 44 per cent of women of working age were in the labour force in 1989, one of the lowest rates of female participation in the European Community. However, women's involvement in paid work has risen steadily since the early 1970s, when only around 33 per cent of working-age women were in the labour force.

The level of self-employment is high, with just over 25 per cent of the labour force in this category. Women make up 36 per cent of the labour force but nearly 60 per cent of the unemployed.

The labour force grew by around 1 per cent during the mid-1980s, but the rate of growth fell back and even became negative at the very end of the decade.

According to Eurostat forecasts, the population in the 15–19 year age group will fall by 16 per cent by the mid-1990s and 30 per cent by the end of the century. The total population of the 15–44 year age group will drop from some 25,500,000 in 1990 to 24,500,000 by the end of the century.

Preparing for recruitment

Informing the authorities

Some of the reporting and official procedures involved in Italian personnel practice might, at first sight, seem formidable. No one should take fright, however, as a good deal of flexibility is permissible when dealing with procedures. One example of this can be seen in a paragraph taken from the *Agenda per l'amministrazione del personale*, the Italian personnel management handbook: it notes that the regulation requiring a list of newly hired workers to be sent to the national social insurance fund (Istituto Nazionale della Previdenza Sociale, INPS) within five days of the hiring, plus a monthly update, can be considered as 'fallen into desuetude' according to government replies to questions in parliament and official communications with the employers' organization Confindustria. Local advice as to which procedures are essential and which can be safely left aside is vital, however.

All employers must provide the Labour Office (l'Ufficio del

Lavoro) and the national social insurance fund, INPS, with the following information:

- The names of people recruited directly under the terms of law No. 264, 9 April 1949, para. 11—a procedure explained below—or recruited in cases of 'urgent necessity' to avoid harm to persons or property (law No. 264/1949, para. 19).
- The name and qualifications of all employees terminating their contracts of employment, within five days of the contract ending.
- The total number employed, broken down by plant, sex and type of work undertaken, as well as the names of people employed who are disabled or who are entitled to compulsory placement. This information must be supplied every six months, in January and June each year.

All employers must also provide the Labour Inspectorate (Ispettorato di Lavoro) with copies of all part-time work contracts within thirty days of the contract commencing.

Work-force consultation

There are no legal obligations on employers to consult trade unions or employee representatives on manpower planning issues or on the recruitment of individuals.

Using part-timers and temps

Part-time and temporary working is less common in Italy than in other EC countries, and accounts for just under 5 per cent of all employment contracts. There is no statutory definition of part-time work other than to say that it is work for fewer hours than those defined in law and by collective agreement as fulltime work. Three types of part-time contracts are currently in use and are permitted, provided they are in writing and a copy is sent to the appropriate provincial labour inspectorate within thirty days of commencement.

They are: 'horizontal' part-time—with a shorter working day than full-time contracts; 'vertical' part-time—where employees work for only part of the week; and 'cyclical part-time'—where employees work for several weeks a month, or several months a year. Failure to notify the inspectorate will entail a fine of L300,000 (£150).

Part-time contracts are regulated mainly by industry or company agreement and part-time workers are entitled *pro rata* to all the benefits enjoyed by their full-time colleagues. They are given priority of consideration for full-time vacancies if desired.

Fixed-term contracts. The law states that all employment contracts are permanent except in given circumstances. Permitted fixed-term contracts, which are regulated by law and collective agreement, must be in writing and a copy must be given by the employer to the employee. They can usually be renewed only once, and in certain circumstances temporary workers are given priority of consideration for full-time vacancies if desired.

Fixed-term contracts are used extensively in tourism and agriculture, and also to cover fluctuations in other industries. They may also be used to cover for absent employees who have the right to return to their jobs, such as those doing military service or on maternity leave, or engaged in other specific, finite tasks.

Temporary agencies have no legal standing in Italy, which has ratified the ILO conventions forbidding private employment agencies. Although some local agencies do exist, the major temporary work agencies familiar to UK practitioners do not operate in Italy because of the legal proscription.

Finding the applicant

Italian law on recruitment begins from the proposition that all placement should take place through the official system. However, there are a number of derogations which effectively allow employers to recruit directly and to select whom they choose, except in the case of semi- and unskilled workers, and the unemployed.

The state placement system

All hirings, except those set out below, have to be approved by the local office of the state placement service (*ufficio di collocamento*) even if the service has played no direct role in finding the new employee. To obtain approval, candidates who have been offered a job must take the appropriate completed form plus their employment record (*libretto di lavoro*)—which also effectively functions as a work permit—to the local placement office, where approval, the *Nulla Osta*, will be given and recorded in the *libretto di lavoro*. Failure to comply with the law can entail penalties ranging from fines of between L1 million (£500) and L5 million (£2,500), or even imprisonment, plus a fine up to a maximum of L15 million (£7,500). We explain below where this procedure is required.

Nearly all employees are covered by national collective agreements laying down minimum terms and conditions. Since collective agreements are legally binding on all employers and employees in the sector concerned, even if they are not signatories to the agreement, recruiters will need to know which agreement operates in their sector. The relevant collective agreement (*contratto collettivo nazionale di lavoro*, CCNL) must be indicated on the form used for obtaining permission to proceed with the engagement of an employee.

Below we set out the somewhat byzantine process for recruiting different types of employee.

Direct recruitment (assunzioni dirette). Direct recruitment on the part of the employer, by advertisement, individual contact or unsolicited application, is possible for the following categories of employees:

- Managers.
- Workers in companies employing no more than three people.
- Workers recruited in an emergency in order to prevent harm to persons or property—if employment exceeds three days, the employer must inform the local placement office of their names, the reason for hire and their terms and conditions.
- Spouses and relatives of the employer (up to second cousins).
- Skilled blue-collar or white-collar staff recruited via open competition, primarily into public employment.

It is not unknown for companies to use small intermediary firms with no more than three people to recruit workers, and then allow them to pass, via a recruitment procedure outlined below, to the ultimate main employer, thereby avoiding some of the constraints of the official system.

Direct passage (passaggio diretto). The placement office will approve the hiring of other categories of employee chosen directly by the employer provided it is done by means of the so-called *passaggio diretto*, in which employees transfer immediately and without interruption from another employer, provided the request is submitted five to six days before the date on which the new employment is scheduled to begin. The following documentation is required: a copy of the previous official approval (*Nulla Osta*), a declaration from the previous employer giving the dates of the previous employment, a copy of the last pay cheque, and the *libretto di lavoro*. Approval is usually granted within ten days, but employment can begin before it arrives.

Recruitment 'by name' (richiesta nominativa). Employees in the following categories can be freely selected by the employer and a 'request by name' made for official approval, which will be granted automatically. Employees may be either employed or currently unemployed or 'between jobs'. We list below only the most important categories of employee to which the procedure applies. It includes:

- White-collar workers or highly skilled (*altamente specializzati*) blue-collar workers.
- Employees aged between 15 and 29 years of age employed on training and work experience contracts lasting no more than twenty-four months.
- Semi- and unskilled workers, provided no more than 50 per cent of an employer's unskilled and semi-skilled work force have already been recruited by this procedure.
- Apprentices, or employees who have completed a training and work experience contract and where the employer makes a request within twelve months of the contract ending.
- Employees who are to be employed on an approved fixed-term contract.

Although the employer has broadly the same prerogative under both *passaggio diretto* and *richiesta nominativa*, there are differences which should be highlighted. Firstly, whereas *passaggio diretto* covers blue or white-collar employees, under *richiesta nominativa* some blue-collar groups are subject to quotas. Secondly, workers recruited via *passaggio diretto* are not part of the 50 per cent quota mentioned above. And thirdly, *richiesta nominativa* allows an employer to recruit someone irrespective of their current employment status, whilst under *passaggio diretto* there cannot even be a day's break between the two employments.

Recruitment 'by number' (richiesta numerica). This represents the true use of the official placement system as the provider of potential employees. It becomes relevant either for employers who have filled their quota of semi-skilled and unskilled workers under the *richiesta nominativa* procedure, or who are unable to find workers to move direct from another employer. Employers looking for a large number of semi- or unskilled workers may also resort to this procedure. The numerical request (*richiesta numerica*) to the official system must state the number of workers required, the qualifications needed, the tasks to be performed, the pattern of working time, and any other terms and conditions. The state agency will send candidates from its lists, the position on the list of the unemployed being determined by social criteria, among other things. Employers can refuse candidates sent by the state agency only if:

- They have previously dismissed them for 'just cause' (*giusta causa*).
- The candidates cannot perform the tasks assigned to them.
- The candidates have failed a previous probationary period with the same employer.
- Candidates fail a medical test.

While the bureaucratic procedures of the state placement office cannot be avoided by employers concerned about their status and image, it is generally recognized by unions and employers alike that the laws governing the hiring of labour are outdated and cumbersome. The official service is not held in high esteem, and recent changes in its structure, designed to meet growing demands from the labour market, have so far had little impact. It has been argued that the existing rules only encourage Italy's already large 'black' economy.

Press advertising

The press is essentially regional in character, although some regional papers, as in Germany, have achieved national status and readership. The main vehicle for job advertisements, *Il Corriere della Sera*, originally based in Milan, now publishes various regional editions and is also printed in Rome. Other important papers with local roots, but a wider readership, which might suggest themselves for managerial and specialist recruitment include *Il Resto del Carlino* in Bologna, *Il Mattino* in Naples, *Il Messaggero* in Rome, *La Repubblica*, also in Rome, and *La Stampa* in northern Italy. More local newspapers can be used for manual and routine white-collar jobs. The main purely business daily, *Il Sole—24 ore*, carries very few job advertisements, although it does play a role in graduate recruitment (see below).

Equal opportunity legislation forbids the specification of gender in job advertisements. However, there are no restrictions on setting age limits. The wording of advertisements has to comply with the Workers' Statute, which forbids discrimination on the grounds of political opinion, race, religion or trade union affiliation. However, employment advertisements never positively assert that an employer is an equal opportunity employer.

Salaries are very rarely mentioned in job advertisements, nor is the company name always stated.

Recruitment consultants

The use of recruitment consultants for selecting candidates of all categories is widespread and growing, particularly in northern Italy, where matching skills to jobs is increasingly difficult. The development of such organizations reflects the lack of an effective official or graduate recruitment infrastructure. Legally, consultants can only advise employers on candidates for jobs, because the actual placement must always be done via the state placement agency. Services provided by recruitment consultants range from merely drafting and placing advertisements in newspapers to shortlisting a number of candidates for final selection by the company concerned. The cost of consultant services would typically be 15 per cent of the candidate's first year's salary plus the cost of the advertisement or 20 per cent of the candidate's first year's salary without an advertisement.

Consultants are allowed to hold files of job seekers.

Executive search

The use of executive search consultants for the recruitment of executives (*dirigenti*) and senior technical staff (*quadri*) has been growing rapidly in recent years, particularly in northern Italy. According to a recent study of the European executive search market carried out by the *Economist*, around 1,000 searches are carried out annually in Italy. Most of the major international executive search organizations are represented in the market, together with smaller local independents.

A number of the larger firms have grouped into a professional association, ACORD (Associazione Italiana tra i Consulenti per la Ricerca Direttiva di Dirigenti), which has set a code of professional ethics to which members have agreed to work. The main points are:

- Confidentiality of information held by ACORD members.
- The client company should not be identified to the candidate without the client's permission, and candidates likewise can be identified to the company only with their prior authorization.
- Assignments can be accepted only if the client provides all the information required about the vacancy and the desired qualifications of the candidate.
- ACORD members must exercise rigorous objectivity when describing clients to candidates, and vice versa.
- Candidates may not be presented to more than one client company at the same time.
- Searches can be carried out only for client employers, and never for executives seeking new jobs.
- No recompense may be accepted from a candidate.
- Client companies may not be approached.
- Assignments can be accepted only on a single-agency basis.

ACORD has no fixed main office but can be reached through the business address of the current president of the association (details in the appendix).

Executives are the only category of employee who may enter into an employment contract directly with the employer. Like other workers, they too are covered by national agreements providing basic minimum terms and conditions, of which all employers need to be aware. In a business environment where lack of employee mobility always appears as a concern to employers, many executives' posts are filled by internal promotion. However, severe shortages in key areas such as engineering and finance have meant a change in this culture and have contributed to the recent growth in the use of executive search consultants. There are no legal restrictions on how these consultants may operate, except for equal opportunity legislation and the Workers' Statute.

Graduate recruitment

There is as yet a relatively undeveloped infrastructure for graduate recruitment in terms of university careers services or recruitment events. Fairs for graduate recruitment do take place but cannot be equated to the 'milk round' operating in the UK. Companies make presentations at the fairs but do not interview there and then. Universities and schools sell lists of their graduates to employers (without the students' permission) and companies who sponsor schools or universities have priority of access to such lists. Students graduate throughout the academic year.

A new initiative in 1990 has been the organizing of an international graduate recruitment event in Milan by AEGEE (Association des Etats Généraux des Etudiants d'Europe), a number of large international firms and *Il Sole—24 ore* at which selected students from throughout Europe have the opportunity to meet potential employers.

Some newspapers, such as the finance and business daily *Il Sole—24 ore* regularly publish lists of graduates from various universities, giving details of the student's name, date of birth, address and telephone number, subject, class of degree, knowledge of languages, whether male, whether or not they have done military service or are exempted, and their preferences regarding location of employment, sector and function. The *Il Sole—24 ore* list is published as a regular supplement in conjunction with Assolombarda, the industrial employers' organization in the Lombardy region around Milan in northern Italy. Information is collected from the universities in Milan, including the Bocconi (business school), the Cattolica, the Statale and the Politecnico, and permission is obtained from new graduates to publish their details.

Unsolicited applications also account for a large proportion of the initial contact between graduates and employers, despite an increasingly tight market for appropriately qualified graduates.

Application documents

Job advertisements typically ask for a detailed C.V., including a telephone number.

The Workers' Statute and equal opportunity legislation forbid employers from putting questions on application forms which seek information about union membership, political opinions, religious beliefs, family situation or pregnancy. There are no other statutory restrictions as to what may be asked. Recruitment specialists within large multinational employers will almost always be expected to adhere to company codes of practice. However, there is no recognized code of practice guiding recruitment and selection procedures comparable with that issued by the Institute of Personnel Management in the UK.

There are no mandatory regulations on how information returned by an applicant may be used. For example, a graphology test could be performed on a handwritten letter without the candidate's express permission. Many consultants, though, would tell candidates if such tests were to be carried out.

Selection

Employers are free to choose their methods of selection, with the precise course of the process determined by the level of vacancy involved. A senior appointment via a recruitment consultant would typically involve, after assessment of C.V.s, three interviews plus tests of various kinds which might involve graphology, psychometric tests and on occasion even physiognomic examination of the candidate's features and skull! For routine white-collar positions, C.V.s would be sorted and those entering the next stage put through an aptitude and/or a job simulation test. There is no obligation to inform applicants about the results of tests, though some employers and consultants will do so.

Provisions in law

What can be asked during an interview is governed, as with application forms, by the Workers' Statute and equal opportunity legislation. It is unlawful to discriminate on grounds of sex either directly—by asking about a candidate's marital status, family circumstances or pregnancy—or indirectly by indicating via pre-selection procedures or the advertisement of vacancies that one sex is required. Nevertheless, more searching questions may be put and expected than is normal in the UK, equal opportunity legislation notwithstanding.

Infringements of the Workers' Statute and equal opportunity legislation are punishable by fines or in extreme cases, theoretically, by imprisonment.

Medical examinations may be asked for by employers prior to engagement. They can be carried out either by a company doctor or an independent physician and the outcome, but not the detailed results, given to the employer. In certain industries, such as food or chemicals, and when recruiting young people, employers are legally required to carry out a medical examination, with the cost borne by the employer.

There is a certain amount of controversy concerning medical examinations, as the Workers' Statute makes them illegal unless undertaken by a doctor in the public service. However, a 1974 ruling of the Constitutional Court stated that this provision applied only to workers already in post, and not to applicants.

Military service currently lasts twelve to fourteen months. When recruiting personnel, it is unlawful to stipulate that candidates should have completed or be exempt from military service. The law also states that employees who undertake military service have a right to reinstatement provided they report back for work within thirty days of discharge. Some national industry agreements, such as retailing and distribution, state that the period spent on military service counts towards seniority.

Employment incentives

The government offers a number of incentives designed to boost youth employment and encourage companies to take workers on in regions of high unemployment. The incentives take two forms: firstly, greater flexibility in employment contracts and hiring procedures, and, secondly, reductions in employers' social security contributions, which are the highest in Europe.

The most important scheme to foster the recruitment of young people aged 15–29, introduced in 1985, offers opportunities for training and work experience contracts. By 1988 nearly 500,000 people were employed on this basis. The scheme allows employers to recruit young people on training and work experience contracts by name—that is, chosen by the employer—even though that particular category of employee would normally be recruited 'by number'. Such contracts must not exceed twenty-four months and are not renewable. The number of young people on such contracts is excluded from the calculation for the quota of employees which are allowed to be recruited by name. In addition, the employer may convert a training and work experience contract into a permanent one and obtain approval for the candidate by name, provided the application is submitted within twelve months of the expiry of the training contract.

Employers recruiting on this type of contract benefit from reduced social security contributions per trainee, as well as being allowed to pay reduced rates of pay. Although national industry rates still apply, trainees can be placed up to two grades below the rate which would have applied on completion of training. Companies are, however, required to provide training schemes which comply with the legislation, and where state or EC funding is sought the schemes must be submitted to the Labour Inspectorate for prior approval.

A bilateral agreement between employers and the major trade unions signed in December 1988 provides additional regulations on training and work experience contracts aimed at establishing limits on the use of these contracts in a given work force. The same agreement, which, it is hoped, will be sanctioned in law, also sets out provisions encouraging the recruitment of other categories of people on temporary contracts.

Eligibility for recruitment on a fixed-term contract includes the unemployed over the age of 29, young people who do not qualify for training and work experience, and young people in areas of high unemployment. Contracts must last at least four months but not more than twelve and no more than 10 per cent of the employer's work force may be employed on such contracts.

The ability to conclude part-time contracts is regarded as an employment incentive under Italian legislation but in 1988 accounted for only 6 per cent of employment contracts, of which 80 per cent were occupied by women.

A five-year plan to boost employment in depressed areas and safeguard international competitiveness in certain industries was introduced in January 1988. Under it some employers in manufacturing industry as well as the craft sector and co-operatives can benefit from reduced social insurance contributions. The plan has recently been the subject of controversy, as the government, prompted by the need to cut public spending, has sought to draw back from financing the scheme. The future of the scheme could be in doubt if the government manages to reform the structure of social security charges as promised.

Employment quotas

There are numerous items of legislation setting quotas for the employment of people with a disability, war invalids, widows and orphans, as well as employment protection for these groups.

In most organizations of more than thirty-five people, at least 15 per cent of the work force should be from one of the following categories (in order of their priority in the legislation):

- Servicemen or women with war disabilities.
- Civilians with war disabilities.
- Persons disabled in military service.
- Persons disabled at work.
- Orphans and widows of those in the above categories.
- Others with disabilities.
- Persons with impaired hearing.

Other people, such as refugees, ex-prisoners of war, and so on, can qualify as one of the above categories as regards recruitment priorities.

Though no positive incentives exist for employers to comply with these quotas, they must make a six-monthly return to the official placement office giving a breakdown of their work force. Employers who fail to meet their obligations can be fined.

Making the offer

The form of the offer

There is no mandatory procedure which employers are constrained to follow when making an offer of employment, though the law does require that it must be in writing if the contract is part-time or fixed-term. Most companies choose to have a written record of the job offer. Some national industry agreements, such as in chemicals, stipulate that the offer must be in writing and must contain the following:

- The date at which employment begins.
- The grade.
- The starting salary.
- The length of any probationary period.
- The place of work.
- All other agreed conditions.

There is no prescribed formula for rejecting candidates.

Work permits and papers

Documents expected of an employee are set down by law and collective agreement. Law No. 112 (10 January 1935) makes it illegal for an employer to engage anyone—with only a few exceptions—who does not have a valid official employment pass (*libretto di lavoro*), which effectively functions as a work permit but also records an employee's work record. Italian and other EC nationals can apply to the local mayor's office (Sindaco) for a *libretto di lavoro*. Other foreign nationals must apply to the Labour Inspectorate.

On engagement, the employer will check the *libretto di lavoro* and retain it during the period of employment. Workers employed by more than one employer must deposit their permit with one employer, who is then required to inform any other employers. On termination of employment the employer must return this document to the employee no later than one day following the end of the employment in return for a receipt from the employee. Employees who have been on training contracts (*contratti di formazione e lavoro*) will have a record of their work and of the training received.

Newly appointed employees will also need to provide a social insurance record, which consists of a block of certificates, one of which is completed each year and sent to the national social insurance fund, INPS, giving details of the preceding year's income.

Some collective agreements also require employees to produce other documentation, such as an identity card (which all Italian citizens carry), proof of eligibility for family allowance, and certificates establishing vocational qualifications. Employees in the metalworking, chemical and pharmaceutical industries also need to keep a health record (*libretto sanitario personale*), which contains information on the results of medical examinations, accidents at work, occupational disease, and absence record through sickness or accident.

Appendix

Organizations

Ministry of Labour and Social
Security (Ministero del Lavoro
e della Previdenza Sociale):
Via Flavia 6
00187 Rome
tel. +39 6 4683

Employment Directorate
(Direzione Generale dei
Rapporti di Lavoro):
as above

AIDP (Italian personnel
managers' association):
Via Cornalia 19
20124 Milan
tel. +39 2 67 09 558

Confindustria (central
employers' organization):
Viale dell'Astronomia 30
0100 Rome
tel. +39 6 59031

ACORD
c/o Proper s.r.l.
Via G. Frua 21/6
20146 Milan
tel. +39 2 48 00 51 12

ASSCO:
Via S. Paolo 10
20121 Milan
tel. + 39 2 79 61 57

Publications

Il Sole—24 ore:
Via Lamazzo 52
20154 Milan
tel. +39 2 31031
fax +39 2 312055

Il Corriere della Sera:
Via Solferino 28
20121 Milan
tel. +39 2 6339

8
Recruitment in the Netherlands

The Netherlands resembles the United Kingdom inasmuch as personnel practitioners can draw on codes of practice—one agreed and the other produced by the personnel management association—to structure recruitment. There is very little statutory regulation of the recruitment process, although collective agreements do make provision on issues such as priority for internal applications.

Demographic change is forecast to hit the Netherlands hard, and women will become a crucial force in balancing supply and demand in the labour market. At present, women's participation in employment is among the lowest in the European Community. The declining number of young people is also highlighting training in a labour market which puts a high value on formal and vocationally specific qualifications.

The labour market

The Netherlands is set to face a particularly severe brush with the demographic time bomb, with official forecasts painting an alarming picture of demographic developments and their implications for the labour market at large. Substantially fewer young people and an increasing number of over-65s are expected to lead to shortages at entry level, although the total work force will grow marginally to the year 2000. By 1996 the number of school and college leavers is expected to have fallen to 120,000 from 173,000 in 1986 for the 16–20 year age group, and to 184,000 from 225,000 in 1986 for the 21–26 year age group.

As elsewhere in Europe, raising women's participation rate will be of fundamental importance in dealing with these shortages. Various measures are currently being implemented to encourage women to remain in employment and to increase the number of returners, with a number of companies running special 'positive action programmes' for women aimed at correcting imbalances between the proportions of men and women in a particular job.

At present a large proportion of women, particularly married women, do not participate in the active labour force. In 1989 the OECD estimated that some 52 per cent of women of working age were in employment, one of the lowest participation rates in the European Community. Both tradition and culture, compounded by a shortage of child care in the 0–4 age group, play a part.

Despite this still comparatively low female participation rate by international standards, the biggest change in labour supply during the past thirty years has been the increase in the percentage of women going out to work: from just 29 per cent in 1973 the rate rose to 40 per cent in 1980, and has continued to increase steadily in recent years.

However, the proportion of women working full-time has declined in the past three years, with the only *overall* increase in women's participation occurring in the age group 30–49. In general the participation rate falls off rapidly between 22 and 30 years of age, then stabilizes or even rises up to 50–55 years, and then falls off steeply again towards retirement age.

Whilst having one of the lowest female participation rates in the European Community, the Netherlands has the highest incidence of part-time work. According to Eurostat, 32 per cent of employees worked part-time in 1987, compared with a Community average of 13 per cent. Women predominate in the part-time work force: 70 per cent of Dutch part-timers were women, accounting for some 55 per cent of all women employees. However, part-time jobs are uncommon in higher functions, with only about 5 per cent of managerial jobs offered on a part-time or job-sharing basis.

Skill levels have risen in recent years, and enhancing the education and competence of the labour force remains a high policy priority. Formal qualifications are important, both in terms of personal status and as a prerequisite for a particular job: relevant work experience is generally not regarded as a substitute for the required qualifications. Graduates are expected to have a degree which is directly relevant to the job they are applying for. A humanities graduate, for example, would find it difficult to embark on a career in retailing, which would normally call for a degree in business studies. Membership of a professional organization, although not obligatory, is often asked for.

Secretarial work is a good example of the importance of formal qualifications. Learning 'on the job' is uncommon, and the minimum requirement is either a completed secretarial course or specific qualifications for the task to be performed: that is, typing, shorthand (Dutch and foreign languages), word processing and business correspondence (Dutch and foreign languages). The central position of the Netherlands in Europe and the country's long-standing international connections place an extra emphasis on the skills of office staff: it is unusual to have a secretary—or indeed any member of the clerical staff—without a knowledge of at least one or two foreign languages in addition to Dutch.

Personnel planning

There is no general legal framework regulating the recruitment and selection of job applicants. Draft legislation was prepared in 1982 but failed to become law. Instead it was agreed that the social partners should mutually agree on a 'correct and proper' procedure, based on the recommendations of the Labour Foundation (Stichting van de Arbeid), a bipartite central forum established in 1945 to facilitate consultation between employers and trade unions. The regulations, which date from 1982 and are dubbed the STAR recommendations, cover recruitment, selection (including interviewing, taking up references and the procedure in using various tests) and the complaints procedure.

The Dutch Institute of Personnel Management (Nederlandse Vereniging van Personeelsbeleid, NVP) also has a code of practice which is along broadly similar lines but offers more detailed and specific guidance on best practice.

We deal with the provisions of both guides at the appropriate point in the recruitment process. Copies of the NVP guide, *NVP sollicitatie code* in Dutch, can be obtained from the NVP address given in the appendix.

Informing the authorities

There is no obligation to inform the labour authorities of vacancies.

According to article 27 of the Act on Works Councils, employers must consult the works council on general issues concerning personnel planning; the works council does not, however, have any influence on individual appointments.

Using part-timers and temps

Temporary work is governed by the law on temporary employment agencies of 1965 (*Wet op ter beschikking stellen van arbeidskrachten*), which stipulates that subcontracting of employees by agencies is subject to a licence from the Minister of Social Affairs. Such a licence is normally refused only if the interests of the workers are insufficiently guaranteed, or if it is feared that subcontracting will impair the overall labour market. There are two kinds of licence: one that covers agencies dealing with office staff, health sector employees and technical draughtsmen and women, and another for agencies dealing with unskilled workers in industry, and trained technical staff.

Agencies are not allowed to assign workers to a client company for longer than six months.

Temporary work has experienced something of a boom in recent years — agencies dealing with temporary work have mushroomed in all cities. During 1988 the number of people in temporary employment increased by 11·1 per cent compared with 1987, and this trend looks set to continue in the 1990s, with employers and workers both looking for ways of making their working life more flexible. An estimated 110,000 people are in temporary employment on any one day. According to official figures, about 73 per cent of all temporary workers are under 30 years of age and some 40 per cent are women.

Temporary workers are covered by a collective agreement which not only deals with general conditions of employment but also sets out guidelines on pay and prescribes minimum hourly rates, based on the statutory minimum wage. The current agreement, which runs until 30 June 1991, also contains a clause which aims to boost temporary workers' salary progression by stipulating that once an employee has worked for 1,000 hours he or she is entitled to a salary increase. Holiday entitlement is at present twenty-five days on an annual basis.

Some collective agreements restrict the use of temporary workers. In banking, they can be taken on only in the following cases: to relieve the seasonal work load, to stand in temporarily in situations involving illness, holidays or a vacancy which has not yet been filled, or to help cover extra work due to structural changes in the organization. In the textile industry, temporary workers may be employed only if an existing vacancy cannot be filled through the 'normal' recruitment channels, or if it is expected that work will not last longer than two months. At Unilever, the food and cosmetics multinational, temporary agencies will be engaged only 'under very special circumstances'. Any agencies engaged must be licensed by the Minister of Social Affairs. In addition the works council is informed at least every six months of any developments and expected trends concerning the use of temporary workers and of those on fixed-term contracts.

Temporary working is forbidden in the construction industry, and there may be other local restrictions.

Fixed-term contracts may be concluded, either by a specified period or until a defined task is completed, as well as to cover for absent workers: in the latter case, the name of the worker being replaced has to be given. Any contract extended by an employer will be deemed to have been renewed for a period identical to the initial contract.

Finding the applicant

There are six main ways of finding a suitable applicant, all of which are used in various proportions. They are, roughly in order of preference:

- Internal recruitment.
- 'Word-of-mouth', with speculative applications very common.
- The state job placement system (Gewestelijk Arbeidsbureau, or GAB).
- Advertisements in newspapers or journals.
- Engaging a recruitment consultant/headhunter.

- Approaching temporary job agencies.

About a third of all collective agreements—which cover almost 80 per cent of the whole work force—have special clauses dealing with recruitment and selection, and some of these clauses set restrictions on the use of temporary workers (see above).

Internal recruitment

Internal recruitment is very much the norm, a factor based on traditional notions of employee loyalty. According to CBS statistics, annual job mobility was at its lowest, 4 per cent, in 1982/83. This figure started increasing only in the late 1980s and is now estimated to be around 15 per cent, measured on an annual basis.

Vacancies are first placed internally on the company's notice boards, and 'internal' application forms are made available. Only if no suitable internal candidate is found will the company embark on external recruitment.

In banking, for instance, the nationwide collective agreement states that internal recruitment must be used before any other means, unless it would be impracticable or it would not be expected to produce the desired result. If a part-time employee wishes to apply for a full-time post which has become vacant in the organization, he or she must be given priority over any external candidates, provided he or she meets all the requirements of the job description. Only if no internal candidates are available will the GAB be notified. Similarly, at Unilever, existing employees are given priority in applying for jobs within the company, prior to external advertising. Each vacancy which cannot be filled through the internal recruitment process will be notified to the GAB.

External recruitment

According to a survey of recruitment approaches published in the June 1990 issue of the personnel management journal *Gids*, the use of the main techniques for external recruitment was as follows:

- Just over 90 per cent of respondents regularly used advertising

in the daily or weekly press for senior and middle-level jobs, and just under 75 per cent for lower-level positions.
- Just under 60 per cent regularly used the state service (GAB) for middle-level positions, and between 75 and 80 per cent used it for lower-level jobs: only 30 per cent used the service for senior positions.
- Word of mouth also played an important part, and was cited by 75 per cent of respondents as a regular method of recruiting into lower-level positions, and by some 55 per cent for higher-level jobs.
- Visiting schools and colleges was next most important, with around 30 per cent making use of this approach for all levels of positions.
- Search and selection bureaux were mentioned as being regularly used by around 30 per cent of respondents, but only for higher-level positions.

We look individually at a number of these approaches below.

State job placement service

The Netherlands has sixty-five regional employment offices, GABs (*gewestelijke arbeidsbureaus*). Their main task is to match supply and demand in the labour market. However, the considerable imbalance between the demand for and supply of labour is leading to a reappraisal of the activities of the GABs to gear them better to market requirements. New legislation to this effect was drafted some ten years ago, but it was only at the end of June 1990 that the Upper House of parliament approved the change in the law, which will be in force from 1 January 1991. This legislation, *Arbeidsvoorzieningswet*, introduces a number of fundamental changes, including the status of the employment offices. At present, job placement is exclusively in the hands of the public authorities. The new legislation stipulates that job placement, as offered by the GABs, will be the joint responsibility of public authorities, employers and employees, who will be represented in equal proportions in a new central organization, the Centraal Bestuur voor de Arbeidsvoorziening (CBA). This national governing body will draw up an outline programme each year, consisting of general guidelines on employment policies throughout the country.

The ban on job placement activities for profit which was introduced in 1930 (*Arbeidsbemiddelingswet 1930*) will be lifted, ending the monopoly of the GABs, which, according to the government, is no longer needed. Private employment agencies are allowed to operate alongside the 'official' job placement system, whose services, as opposed to those of any private agencies, will continue to be free of charge.

Present standing of the employment offices and their services. The image and efficiency of the GABs have been the main focus of an ongoing debate concerning the role of these offices in the labour market. Employers are not required to notify the GAB of any vacancies, and indeed very few do so. In 1988 only about a third of *all* vacant jobs were reported to the GABs, and of these only around 10 per cent were ultimately filled through the services provided by the GAB. In an effort to improve their image, the employment offices are developing closer partnership with employers across the whole area of personnel planning. Besides selection, the GABs' services include information on employment contracts, advice on dismissal procedures, and training programmes. The GABs are particularly concerned with the training of unemployed people or of those threatened with unemployment. Priority is given to unemployed youths, women, ethnic minorities and the long-term unemployed.

State placement services for the employer. GABs keep a databank of vacancies, with details of the job, the employer (who can remain anonymous), and in some offices of job-seekers, or in any case a card index or on-line terminals. After pre-selecting a number of candidates the GAB will help the employer further in the selection process by arranging interviews and eventual tests.

Unemployed job seekers who want to draw unemployment benefit must register with the GAB.

Recruitment consultancies

Recruitment consultancies have gained in importance over the past few years. An estimated 25 per cent of all middle-ranking and top management posts are now filled through consultancies or executive search bureaus. Around 360 recruitment consultancies, many of which have only one or two consultants, are currently active, some specializing in a specific area or profession. A typical minimum annual salary level for a post that merits engaging a recruitment consultancy is around fl. 60,000 (£18,000) while executive search bureaux usually handle assignments with a minimum annual remuneration around fl. 80,000–100,000 (£25,000–30,000).

Fees charged by consultancies vary, but are typically around 15–20 per cent of the annual salary, depending on which search method is used and how difficult the placement is expected to be. A top management search will cost 30 per cent of the executive's annual salary. Some consultancies have a 'no cure — no fee' policy while others charge an initial, non-refundable fee, usually in the region of fl. 3,000–5,000.

Some consultancies operate a 'guarantee' scheme under which a client is contacted six months after the appointment to see whether the selected candidate has proved to be a success.

The professional body for consultancies is OAWS (Organisatie van Adviesbureaux voor Werving en Selectie), established in 1983. At present it has seventy-six member companies, including executive search bureaux, operating in the field of recruitment and selection of middle and top management.

The OAWS has a code of practice which all member companies must work to. It requires the following:

- A member company must seek to avoid any action which might harm the profession's image.
- Members must not accept any payment in any form from anyone except the client. Under no circumstances is a member allowed to accept payment from an individual looking for work.
- Members must regard all information they receive while performing their task as confidential, and must not give any information which they know or think to be incorrect to others.
- Members must ensure that all parties involved respect this confidentiality. They are not allowed to part with any personal data except within the scope of the assignment.
- Members must remain objective in their assessment of the candidates.
- Each member will keep files of personal data only if the person in question has given their permission. These details must not

be given to a third party without the prior permission of the candidate. Permission must be obtained again if the candidate is going to be assessed for any other vacancy.
- Members should not contact candidates who have already been placed for an appointment elsewhere unless the client specifically asks the consultant to do so. This rule holds for a minimum of two years following the completion of the previous assignment.
- Members must confirm *in writing* all details concerning the assignment. This confirmation must include: description of the search method to be used, the search fee, overheads, the method of payment, the estimated time necessary and the name of the individual consultant who will be dealing with the assignment. The written confirmation must also state that the consultant will be working according to the OAWS code of conduct.
- Members may accept an assignment only if the client is able to guarantee that no other consultancy has been approached for the same post; on the other hand, more than one consultancy can be engaged to handle separate assignments from the same client.

A full list of member companies and their specialist areas of recruitment, together with global details of fees charged, is available from OAWS (see appendix).

Advertising in the media

Although the Saturday supplements of the newspapers seem to be filled with job advertisements—21 per cent of all advertising space in 1989 was taken up by recruitment advertising—employers do not rate direct advertising as an especially effective method.

The Netherlands has around 250 recognized advertising agencies, and about ten of these specialize in recruitment. However, the vast majority of employers draft their job advertisements themselves.

Part of the Dutch personnel managers' code covers advertising. Advertisements must contain relevant and accurate information on the essential characteristics of the vacant post, such as:

- Tasks and duties, specifying particular areas of responsibility if applicable.
- The location of the company and the workplace.
- The hours of work, with an indication of whether they involve unsocial hours or shift work.
- If the job is for a fixed period only, the time limit must be specified.
- If psychological testing will be a part of the selection process the advertisement must state as much; similarly, if the works council is going to be consulted it must be evident from the text.
- The closing date for applications as well as the estimated time necessary to complete the selection (preferably not exceeding three months).
- The name and telephone number of the contact person who can supply additional information on the vacant post.

The NVP code of practice states that, unless there is a particular reason for not doing so, an advertisement should have an indication of the expected salary. In practice, however, salaries are usually mentioned for public sector posts only, while the rest use expressions like 'competitive' or 'good'.

The NVP code of practice does not include any provisions limiting the specification of age limits and most jobs advertised in the media have a preferred age range; many set an absolute upper age limit.

Advertisements must not contain:

- False or misleading statements on the nature of the job, the salary or the place of work.
- Discriminatory requirements in relation to race, nationality, marital status, religious conviction or sex.

The advertisement should also indicate whether the procedure will be carried out in accordance with the NVP code, or whether it will entail another procedure developed by the recruiting company.

Most national and regional newspapers carry job advertisements, often in a Saturday supplement (papers do not appear on Sundays). The *NRC Handelsblad*'s 'Zaterdags Bijvoegsel' (Saturday supplement) carries job ads for posts at a high level such as for directors, general managers, economists, lawyers, international executives, heads of section and PR appointments. Job advertisements in the *Algemeen Dagblad* are aimed more at middle management in sales, marketing, construction, computing and social work. The *Volkskrant* attracts ads mainly from employers in the health sector and education, as well as those in the public sector. *Intermediair Weekblad*, a weekly paper distributed to new graduates and students in their final year, has job ads in all sectors, with emphasis on junior rather than senior management functions. The *Economisch Dagblad*, a business daily, has job ads mainly for economists and higher personnel in banking and finance.

Some specialist journals carry advertisements. For jobs in engineering and engineering management there is *PT Aktueel*, and for jobs in the advertising industry *Adformatie*. Vacancies in personnel are found above all in *PW* and *Personeelsbeleid*, both monthly journals. Management jobs in the building and construction industry are advertised in *Bouw*, a twice-monthly journal.

Graduate recruitment

A special official job placement system for university graduates was introduced in the 1970s but most graduate placements are handled centrally and not through the regional offices. Owing to the small size of the regional labour market for the different categories of university graduates, there is little incentive for the staff in regional employment offices to deepen their knowledge and insight of this specialist market. The overall number of university graduates placed through the state system remains low.

The central state graduate service, the *Bureau Arbeidsvoorziening Academici*, publishes two guides in the area of graduate recruitment: *Vacant* carries vacancies, and *Sollicitant* includes details of graduates seeking employment.

Although most universities have a careers advice service, only a handful have a more developed placement infrastructure. Those that have include the business schools at Rotterdam and Nijenrode. Students' organizations may organize local recruitment events.

Selection

According to the recruitment survey carried out by the journal *Gids*, the most prevalent selection techniques cited were:

- Interviewing was the prime technique, cited by between 95 and 100 per cent for all grades of employee.
- Around 95–100 per cent also used the letter of application.
- Between 60 and 70 per cent regularly used information collected via an application form.
- References were taken up by around 70 per cent of employers for senior-level appointments, but by less than 50 per cent for lower-level appointments.
- Psychological tests were very frequently used for senior appointments in 40 per cent of firms, and regularly used at this level by nearly 60 per cent.
- Less than 10 per cent of respondents used assessment centres, graphology or astrology.
- A test of competence was carried out regularly by around 30 per cent of respondents for lower-level jobs, but by less than 10 per cent for higher-level appointments.
- Medical examination was cited by around 90 per cent of employers.

Initial selection is usually on the basis of a letter of application, an application form, or both. In small firms it is not uncommon to have a preliminary discussion with candidates on the telephone before inviting them to interview. It is not customary to acknowledge all applications; usually only those who are invited to interview will be notified. (This is sometimes indicated in the advertisement.) Invitations to an interview usually state the name(s) and function(s) of those who will be present at the interview; companies may also indicate the procedure for reimbursing travel costs, the estimated duration of the interview and whether any tests are expected to be set before or during the interview.

The interview. According to the STAR (Stichting van de Arbeid) recommendations, an employer is expected to supply information about the organization, the job itself, the salary and other conditions of employment as well as about opportunities for development and training, and promotion prospects within the company. If references are to be taken up, the current employer will be approached only if the candidate has no objection. The STAR guidelines also stipulate that candidates who are rejected at this point should be sent a letter as soon as possible, with some indication of the reasons for rejection.

An interviewer may ask any questions considered 'relevant' to the job. Many employers interpret this very broadly indeed and specific questions on applicants' health (including details of their GP), marital status, number of children, spouse's name, age and job are frequently asked.

Additional selection criteria. References are usually taken up only in the case of middle and high-ranking appointments. In most cases it will be with the consent of the applicant, but cases have been known of a company approaching organizations without the candidate's permission. Psychological testing and graphology are used almost only for managerial posts, while medical examination is a standard part of the selection procedure at all function levels. Checking criminal records is uncommon. It is worth noting that in about half of all cases where psychological testing or graphology has been used, the candidate will receive a summary of the main findings. This is less customary with the medical, which tends to be only a routine check-up, usually geared to the requirements of company pension schemes, which are widespread in the Netherlands.

Making the offer

There is no statutory procedure concerning how the job offer is made to the selected candidate. The STAR guidelines state that the chosen candidate should be offered a written employment contract, which would contain general conditions of employment, salary, the length of any probationary period and the period of notice, with any other specific provisions agreed during the interview. The candidate should receive two copies, sign both and return one to the employer, keeping the other for their own file.

In practice virtually all companies make use of a written contract of employment and a majority will also include the matters discussed and agreed during the interview.

Handling rejected applicants

The STAR guidelines set out a recommended procedure for dealing with rejected applicants. They should, according to the STAR, be sent a letter explaining, not necessarily in detail, the reasons for rejection. Any documents the applicant submitted, including copies of diplomas, and references should be returned unless the applicant has specifically indicated that the company may keep them. If a personality test has been carried out as part of the selection procedure the report and results should be returned to the psychologist involved.

All rejected applicants are in practice usually notified of the decision, in most cases by a letter but often, in smaller firms, by telephone. Such communication takes place normally within a week or ten days of the decision being made. According to a survey by COB, some 70 per cent of larger firms send out an explanatory letter with an outline of the reasons for rejection. Only about half the smaller firms do this. In about two-thirds of such cases a personalized letter is drafted, while a quarter of the companies surveyed used a standard letter.

Grievances

There is no set formula for handling grievances, although complaints are not entirely unknown. The STAR guidelines recommend that an independent body should be available to handle any grievances. In practice, however, there is no such body. Instead, grievances are usually tackled by the personnel manager.

Appendix

Organizations

Ministry of Social Affairs and
Employment (Ministerie van
Sociale Zaken en
Werkgelegenheid):
Postbus 20801
2600 EV 's-Gravenhage
tel. +31 70 371 5911
fax +31 70 371 4555

Dutch Association of Personnel
Managers (Nederlandse
Vereniging van
Personeelsbeleid, NVP):
Catharijnensingel 53
Postbus 19124
3501 DC Utrecht
tel. +31 30 367101 (membership
enquiries), 367155 (training),
367137 (administration)

Organisatie van Adviesbureaus
voor Werving en Selectie
(OAWS) (recruitment
consultants' association):
Postbus 5451
1007 AL Amsterdam
tel. +31 30 5737800

Nederlandse Instituut van
Psychologen (NIP):
Postbus 5362
1007 AJ Amsterdam
tel. +311 20 791526

Algemene Bond
Uitzendondernemingen (ABU):
Koningslaan 34
1075 AD Amsterdam
tel. +31 20 5738783

Commissie Ontwikkeling
Bedrijven van de Sociaal-
Economische Raad (COB/SER)
(Social and Economic Council):
Postbus 90405
2509 LK 's-Gravenhage
tel. +31 70 3499 499

Stichting van de Arbeid (Labour
Foundation):
Postbus 90405
2509 LK 's-Gravenhage
tel. +31 70 349 9648

Netherlands–British Chamber of
Commerce:
Holland Trade House
Bezuidenhoutseweg 181
2594 AH 's-Gravenhage
tel. +31 70 478881
fax +31 70 477975

Publications

Algemeen Dagblad:
Westblaak 180
Rotterdam 2
London agent: Joshua Powers Ltd
46 Keyes House
Dolphin Square
London SW1V 3NA
tel. 071-834 5566

NRC Handelsblad:
Westblaak 180
Rotterdam 2
London agent: as for *Algemeen Dagblad*

Bouw:
Weena 700
PO box 299
3000 AG
Rotterdam

Gids (Journal of Personnel Management):
Postbus 23
7400 GA Deventer
tel. +31 5700 48999
fax +31 5700 11504

Intermediair:
London office
Publimedia Ltd
The White House
Roxby Place
Ricket Street
London SW6 1RS
tel. 071-381 8427

Personeelbeleid (journal of the NVP):
Postbus 19124
3501 DC Utrecht
tel. 030 367101

9
Recruitment in Portugal

Although recruitment itself is not highly regulated, other areas of employment—and in particular dismissal—are complex. Recent legislation has introduced new rules for temporary work and fixed-term contracts.

Rapid economic growth in recent years has pushed registered unemployment down to one of the lowest levels in the European Community. Shortages of managers, specialists and skilled manual workers are creating problems for recruiters and pushing up pay levels, although labour costs remain low compared with the EC average. Local personnel professionals expect recruitment to get harder over the next two years.

There are particular shortages of senior managers, especially in the north, electrical engineers, data-processing specialists, finance and accountancy people and marketing specialists. Labour shortages and the need for training have generated a substantially increased demand for human resource managers.

Outstanding features of the recruitment scene include:

- Relatively low interregional mobility, though congestion in Lisbon may be raising willingness to relocate.
- A need to develop policies to retain skilled people after training.
- Agencies for permanent as well as temporary placement are permitted.

The labour market

The labour force in 1988 stood at some 4,600,000 persons, out of a population of working age of 6,450,000. This participation rate of 72 per cent is the highest in southern Europe by some margin, and higher than the OECD European average of 66 per cent. Much of this is attributable to the high level of women's participation in paid work, which at 59 per cent, is also above the EC average, and only slightly below the rate for the UK. Some 22 per cent of the total labour force, and 27 per cent of women, still work in agriculture.

Part-time work, as measured by Eurostat in 1987, accounted for only 4·3 per cent of employees, and 6·3 per cent of the total labour force: 67 per cent of part-timers were women.

According to Eurostat population projections the 15–19 year age group is set to shrink from 877,000 in 1991 to 739,000 by the year 2001. The number of live births fell from a peak of 179,000 a year in 1976 to 126,000 by 1986. However, the 15–44 age group will continue to grow at least until the end of the century.

Personnel planning

Consulting the authorities

There is no statutory obligation to consult the authorities on matters of recruitment above and beyond requirements to ensure that new employees are correctly registered for tax and social security purposes.

Consulting the work force

Under legislation on workers' committees (*comissões de trabalhadores*) dating from 1979 (legislative decree 46/79), work-force representatives have a broad right to information which they require to carry out their function and participate in the management and restructuring of their enterprise. There is a specific right to information on personnel management and policies, but no obligation as such to consult either on individual hiring decisions or on such issues as guidelines for selection. Workers' committees may be established by employees in any enterprise, and are elected by proportional representation. They exist in parallel with trade union representation.

Collective agreements, which can operate at sectoral or enterprise level, frequently require the internal advertising of posts, and also set out procedures for regrading and promotion. Especially in public enterprises—some of which face privatization—collective agreements may also regulate recruitment and selection criteria, together with minimum agreed qualifications for specific positions.

Using part-timers and temps

There are no specific regulations governing the use of part-timers. Part-timers enjoy the same basic rights as other employees, and must be paid the proportion of the appropriate full-time remuneration which corresponds to their hours of work. Employers who want to introduce part-time employment would need to obtain the views of the workers' committee in their establishment, should one exist, before making any changes in hours of work. Employees with children under 12 may apply to work part-time for a period of up to three years followed by reinstatement as a full-time employee under parental protection legislation passed in 1984.

Important new legislation regulating the situation of workers on fixed-term contracts and temporary workers was introduced in 1989.

Legislative decree 64–A/89 (27 February 1989) sets out new conditions for *fixed-term contracts*. Fixed-term contracts may be concluded only for:

- The temporary replacement of a worker who, for any reason, is prevented from rendering service or against whom legal proceedings regarding the consideration of lawful dismissal are pending.
- A temporary or exceptional increase in the enterprise's activities.
- Seasonal work.
- The accomplishment of an occasional task or specified service of a precisely defined and non-enduring character.
- The launching of a new activity of uncertain duration or the commencement of activity in an enterprise.
- The execution, direction and supervision of operations in civil construction works, public works, industrial building and maintenance.
- The development of projects, including planning, research, direction and supervision, which are not a customary part of the employer's activity.

- Hiring workers for their first job or the long-term unemployed.

Fixed-term contracts must be in writing, signed by both parties, and set out the employee's skill or qualification, remuneration, the established duration and the reason for the contract. Failure to do this could mean that the contract is deemed to have been concluded for an indefinite term.

In the case of temporary replacement, seasonal work, civil and public works and project development, the contract may be concluded for an unspecified term, with the contract ending when the task at hand has been accomplished.

The probationary period within which either side may withdraw is fifteen days for a contract not exceeding six months, thirty days for a contract between six months and two years, and sixty days if the contract is for longer than two years.

A fixed-term contract subject to renewal may not be repeated more than twice, and the total duration of the contracts may not exceed three successive years. In the case of a contract for launching a new activity the maximum length is two years. Employment which exceeds the agreed period and where the renewal has occurred more than twice or has gone beyond three successive years will be deemed to be indefinite.

The employer must notify the worker at least eight days before the expiry of the contract that he does not wish to renew it. Failure to do so where the contract has not been renewed twice, or three years have elapsed, will entail a renewal of the contract for a term at least equal to the period of the first contract. At least three months must have elapsed between the end of one period of fixed-term employment exceeding twelve months and the hiring of a new employee in that same position.

Temporary work via temporary agencies is now regulated by legislative decree 358/89 (17 October 1989). This law provides for the authorization of employment agencies and specifies the circumstances under which temporary workers may be used. Temporary workers remain employees of the agency. Contracts between agency and employee may be open-ended or fixed-term. Agencies which meet the criteria set out by the law may apply for authorization from the Ministry of Labour and Social Security. Amongst other things, agencies have to deposit a sum equivalent to 150 times the statutory minimum monthly wage with the state employment and training agency IEFP (Instituto do Emprego e Formação Profissional).

From the user's point of view, temporary workers may be used under the following circumstances; in each case, there is a maximum permitted period for an individual to carry out the designated activity at the designated workplace:

- To replace an absent worker or a worker unable to render service (may not exceed specified purpose).
- To fill a post during recruitment for that position (maximum of six months).
- To meet temporary or exceptional increase in activity (twelve months).
- A well defined and non-enduring task (twelve months).
- For seasonal activities (six months).
- To meet intermittent needs for labour during whole days or parts of days, provided that the weekly use of temporary labour does not exceed the normal period of work in the establishment (six months, but renewable until the task is complete).
- To allow the establishment to implement projects of a limited duration which are not part of its regular activity, such as installation, repair and maintenance (six months, but renewable until the task is complete).

The contract between the temporary work agency and the client company must be in writing and must indicate:

- The names and head offices of the two parties.
- The numbers of employees in each enterprise contributing to the social insurance system.
- The reasons for the use of temporary work.
- The nature of the post to be filled.
- The location.
- Hours of work.
- Remuneration.
- The start and duration of the contract.
- Whether it is for a specified or unspecified duration.
- The date on which the contract was concluded.

Where a workers' committee exists, it must be informed of the use of any temporary workers in the establishment.

Employees working on a temporary basis are subject to the client company's work regime, including health and safety, and temporary employees must have access to social facilities.

Most of the international majors operate agencies in Portugal, and some companies have grouped themselves into an association, known as APETT, which issues a code of conduct for members.

Finding the applicant

Employers may either opt to use the official placement system (IEFP), go to one of the authorized agencies for the permanent placement of workers which are allowed to operate in Portugal, or advertise directly.

The official placement system

This is administered by the state employment and training agency IEFP. IEFP is an autonomous public body with a tripartite management board, and reports to the Ministry of Labour and Social Security. It has broad responsibilities for the supervision of the labour market, including training and placement, for which it operates employment centres throughout the country.

The service is used by employers looking for manual workers but has a mixed reputation, and efforts are currently under way to improve its effectiveness, especially in the provision of training and the supply of skilled workers to the labour market. Considerable sums are also being made available through the EC's European Social Fund to combat the shortage of industrial skills caused by the lack of effective employer training schemes, and to tackle issues such as rural illiteracy.

The comparatively low level of unemployment has reduced the pool of available labour, and many of the unemployed registered with IEFP tend to be less likely to meet the needs of employers.

Incentives are available for companies who hire candidates from the state system, including grants in some regions and exemptions from social insurance contributions for up to two years.

Private agencies

Private agencies for permanent placement are allowed to operate, and are subject to an authorization procedure set out in legislative decree 124/89 (14 April 1989). Agencies are not permitted to place foreign nationals lacking a valid residence permit in employment, nor to place a Portuguese employee in employment abroad.

Agencies are used for all categories of employee, but most frequently for specialists and in executive search and selection and less commonly for blue-collar positions. Agencies can undertake all stages of the recruitment process, from inserting and designing advertisements to pre-selection, testing, and drawing up a short list or offering an individual candidate. Companies may place their own advertisements but use the testing facilities of an agency.

Although still not the norm, the use of agencies for advertising and selection is a rapidly growing practice and is adopted by large companies, perhaps tackling new areas of the market for the first time, as well as small.

One survey carried out by an independent consultant found that seventy agencies had placed at least one job advertisement in the national press over a one-year period. A number of major groupings, including the larger international auditing and consulting organizations, and recruitment specialists such as the French-headquartered Egor group, operate in the Portuguese market, as well as established local organizations.

Press advertising

The main national vehicle for specialist and management appointments is the newspaper *Expresso*, published on Saturdays. The appointment supplement contains up to twenty pages of job advertisements. The Lisbon-based daily *Diário de Notícias* carries a substantial number of advertised vacancies. The more popular morning daily *Correiro da Manhã* also carries job advertisements, especially for skilled and unskilled staff in services. For employers located in the north the *Commercio do Porto* carries jobs primarily for Oporto and the surrounding region. Regional or local dailies can be used to find both blue-collar and technical staff.

Job advertisements, according to sex equality legislation, 'may not either directly or indirectly contain any restriction, specification or preference based on sex'.

Salaries are only very rarely indicated. Age ranges are given. Smaller companies looking for skilled blue-collar employees often use a box number rather than advertise under their own name. However, this would not be normal practice for companies seeking to establish a presence or reputation in the labour market.

Managerial recruitment

Managerial recruitment can take place via advertising, direct approach by the potential employer or through an agency. A number of employment agencies carry out both executive search and selection as well as more general recruitment. There are also specialist executive search and selection consultants, including some of the European majors, the large auditors, and long-established local independents. There is no association of executive search consultancies as such, although some firms may belong to APPC, the trade association for management consultants.

There is no code of practice, and conduct is guided either by company practice or the imperatives of commercial common sense. However, off-limits rules may differ between companies, with some firms never returning to look for candidates in a client company whereas others may return after a time limit. Firms may directly approach candidates. Files or databases can be kept, but the Portuguese constitution gives the individual a right of access and limits third-party access.

The shortage of managers, combined with the rapidly growing economy and an influx of foreign direct investment, has created a tight market for executive talent, and salaries at top management level have been rising strongly in recent years.

Fee practice for a search varies from 30 per cent of first-year salary for the high-profile internationally operating consultants, to either 20 per cent, or 15 per cent plus advertising costs, for some smaller local independents. A selection operation alone would cost approximately 15 per cent of first year's salary.

Recruiting graduates

Graduate recruitment is characterized by a fairly high degree of informality and unsolicited applications from students to employers. Universities do not, in general, have a developed careers service, and regular recruitment fairs are not part of the scene. One of the first recruitment fairs to be held was organized in the engineering faculty at Lisbon University in 1990. Private universities account for around 25 per cent of those in higher education.

Firms often contact universities to obtain a list of graduates, and student associations also send lists to employers. Companies may cultivate individual contacts with faculty members.

Work placements for students with companies are beginning to develop, and may grow further at the instigation of employers—especially from outside Portugal—who are accustomed to a closer relationship with university departments.

University students entering the work force will be aged around 24–25. About 10–20 per cent of students do military service, with those studying subjects which represent shortage areas for the private sector, such as engineering, tending to be called up. Young people leave school at 18 for matriculation, and degree courses typically last four or five years. Military service, currently eighteen months, may be substantially reduced in the near future.

Application documents

Most advertised positions for managers and specialists simply call for a C.V. and in some cases a recent photograph. Employers customarily ask for copies of educational or professional certificates later in the recruitment process.

Employers are required on request to give departing employees a statement establishing their employment. The Ministry of Labour and Social Security also issues a document, known as a *carteira profissional*, which records the attained qualification of a number of specialized professionals, but not the bearer's employment record. This may also be relevant for grading employees under collective agreements.

Selection

The interview is the prime selection technique but testing of various sorts is a growing and accepted part of the recruitment process.

Psychometric and aptitude testing is carried out by many consultancies, either as part of a complete recruitment assignment or as a specific service to an employer. It is widely accepted by candidates up to middle management level, but not for senior managers. Graphological tests are used by some consultancies in conjunction with interviews for senior managers, although the practice is not as widespread as in France. There is no requirement to obtain a candidate's permission before submitting a handwritten application for graphological test, nor any obligation—beyond good practice—to divulge the results of this or any other test. Assessment centres are rare, but growing.

Privacy provisions

Interviewers may not ask questions about an individual's family circumstances or marital status. Questions must not enable employers to discriminate on grounds of sex, race, ideology, political beliefs or country of origin. Nevertheless, despite these constitutional guarantees, a non-Portuguese human resources manager of a large multinational employer whose own training and home environment had 'trained them not to ask' expressed surprise at candidates' expectations of the sorts of subjects which an interview might touch on.

A woman may not be asked in an interview whether she is pregnant, unless the position involves work for which health and safety regulations forbid the employment of pregnant women.

Medical examinations may be carried out prior to engagement. Doctors are only permitted to declare whether a candidate meets the standard required and is fit or not-fit for the designated task. They may not divulge detailed results of an examination to a third party without the candidate's permission.

The issue of HIV is a subject of concern to practitioners, as it raises delicate and potentially explosive questions of medical confidentiality and definitions of fitness. As yet, however, there is little experience or case law to guide employers. Practitioners feel that at present a doctor would be likely to declare an HIV+ person fit for work in most occupations.

Asking for a candidate's *criminal record*—for example, on an application form—is not an invariable part of the recruitment process, but would be expected in any positions where security or responsibility for money were involved. Candidates may demand a copy of their criminal record (*registo criminal*) from the Centro de Identificação Civil e Criminal: it lists criminal convictions but not minor misdemeanours or spent offences, the period for which varies according to the nature of the conviction. Identity papers, issued by the same office, are carried by all citizens.

Anti-discrimination provisions

The Portuguese constitution forbids discrimination on grounds of sex, race, country of origin, ideology or religious belief.

Legislative decree 392/79 (20 September 1979) provides for equality of opportunity and treatment for women and men in employment. As already noted, this forbids the advertising of job vacancies in a form which might be discriminatory. This law also requires recruitment to be carried out according to objective criteria, and stipulates that 'it shall be unlawful to specify physical requirements unrelated to the occupation or the conditions in which it is carried on' (article 7.2). Exceptions are permitted in work connected with the fashion industry, the arts and entertainment.

Offer and acceptance

The form of the offer

There are no statutory requirements on forms or procedures for making a job offer, and companies are not required to send a notice of rejection within a prescribed period of time. Nor is there any requirement as regards the form in which acceptance has to be confirmed. Employers do, however, usually make an offer in writing.

Work permits

Portugal is still in its transitional period of entry into the European Community, and this also imposes some limitations on the free circulation of workers, with prior authorization required for employment. These transitional arrangements are due to end as from 1 January 1993.

During the transitional period, both residence and work permits will continue to be required, and the starting point for this official procedure is an application to the nearest Portuguese consulate in the applicant's country of residence. Employers already operating in Portugal who want to bring in a UK, or other national, can apply to the Ministry of Labour, and must demonstrate that the proposed function can only be satisfactorily carried out by the non-Portuguese citizen.

Appendix

Organizations

The Ministry of Labour and Social Security (Ministério do Emprego e da Segurança Social):
Praça de Londres 2
Lisbon
tel. +351 1 80 44 60

Institute of Employment and Vocational Training (Instituto do Emprego e Formação Profissional) (administers the state placement system):
11 avenue José Malhoa
Lisbon
tel. +351 1 726 25 36

Association of Portuguese Human Resource Managers (Associação Portuguesa dos Gestores e Técnicos dos Recursos Humanos, the professional organization of personnel practitioners, a member of the European Association of Personnel Management and the World Federation of Personnel Management Associations. Founded in 1964, it has 2,000 individual members. Companies may also affiliate to the association):
avenue do Brasil, 194, 7°
1700 Libson
tel. +351 1 89 97 66
fax +351 1 80 93 40

Office in Oporto:
rua Formosa, 49 1º
tel. +351 2 32 32 34
fax +351 2 200 07 64

Confederation of Portuguese Industry (Confederação da Industria Portuguesa, CIP, the central employers' organization for industry):
avenue 5 de Outubro, 35 1º
1000 Lisbon
tel. +351 1 54 74 54

Confederation of Portuguese Commerce (Confederação do Comércio Porguguës, the central employers' organization in trade and commerce):
rua Saraiva de Carvalho, 1º
1000 Libson
tel. +351 1 66 85 39

APETT (Association of Temporary Employment Agencies):
c/o Marcelina Pena Costa
rua Quirino da Fonseca 15
1000 Lisbon
tel. +351 1 57 04 15

APPC (Associação Portuguesa de Projectistas e Consultores):
Management consultants organization
avenue Antonio Augusto Aguiar 126–7º
1000 Lisbon
tel. +351 1 52 04 76
(member of FEACO)

British–Portuguese Chamber of Commerce:
rua da Estrela 8
1200 Lisbon
tel. +351 1 60 44 00
fax +351 1 60 15 13

Publications

Expresso:
rua Duque de Palmela 37–3º
Lisbon
tel. +351 1 352 61 41

Diário de Notícias:
avenue da Liberdade 266
1200 Lisbon
tel. +351 1 56 11 51
fax +351 1 53 66 27

10
Recruitment in Spain

Recruitment in Spain is still marked by relics of the corporate state, and in a number of areas the law is a good deal more rigid than that in the United Kingdom. However, measures intended to combat persistently high unemployment have created the possibility of extensive resort to part-time work and fixed-term contracts, and in 1988 just over half of all new hirings were carried out under employment schemes.

Rapid economic growth in the second half of the 1980s has put pressure on areas of the labour market, despite high unemployment, and there has been high demand, with consequent pay pressures for managers and specialists. Local practitioners highlight the following issues:

- Rigid employment legislation in aspects of hiring and dismissal.
- A low level of employee mobility between regions.
- Shortages of suitably qualified graduates.

The labour market

Spain's labour force in 1988 stood at some 14,900,000 out of a population of working age of 25,655,000. The overall participation rate, at 59 per cent, is the lowest in the European Community. Female participation, at around 40 per cent, is also the lowest bar the Irish Republic.

Although economic growth was above the EC average during the 1980s, it was not sufficient to offset rapid growth in the labour force, much of which is attributable to an increase in women's involvement in paid work. Although still low by EC standards, female participation rose from 33 per cent to 40 per cent between 1983 and 1989.

Part-time work, as measured by Eurostat, accounted for only 5 per cent of employees, of which 76 per cent were women.

Although the population aged 15–44 is expected to increase modestly by the year 2000, the 15–19 age group will fall quite substantially from 3,285,000 in 1990 to 2,492,000 by the end of the century. The number of births fell from a 1970s peak of 686,000 in 1974 to reach only 460,000 by the mid-1980s.

Personnel planning

In principle, employers are able to recruit freely. However, certain restricting factors do exist, partly as an inheritance of Francoist labour market controls and partly as a reflection of the conditions of rising unemployment which prevailed when the current legislation on employment contracts was devised in the late 1970s and early 1980s. Spanish employers' most often heard criticism is that the labour market is too rigid.

Article 38 of the 1978 constitution guarantees the employer freedom of action in the labour market. Under the centralized and bureaucratic Francoist legislation on hiring and firing, regulations even went so far as to stipulate the number of employees on each grade in a company. Current legislation does not directly address the issues of the structure of the work force or procedures for filling vacancies, except in special cases such as regulations for employing disabled employees or for employing workers on subsidized job-creation contracts.

Work-force consultation

An element of employee participation was introduced in article 64 of the Workers' Statute (law 8/1980), which grants works committees the right to receive quarterly reports on recruitment plans, to express their views before the employer restructures the work force or effects redundancies or lay-offs and, finally, to issue a report before any merger, take-over or change in the legal status of the company which would affect the work force. In addition, article 85 of the Workers' Statute provides a wide range of powers within collective bargaining, including provisions on the size of the work force in the sense that the employer will guarantee to maintain the size of the work force during the period of a collective agreement. Such clauses are not common in the private sector, however.

Employee representation in the recruitment process was strengthened by an agreement reached in January 1990 between the government and the two main union confederations, the UGT (socialist-affiliated) and CC.OO (communist-led). Legislation proposed under the agreement would require employers to give workers' representatives a copy of all employment contracts issued—a step designed to combat widespread fraud in the recruitment process. Employers would also be obliged to transmit plans on personnel planning and recruitment to these representatives. Such plans would also include forecasts of new contracts and the type of contracts issued. Legislation on this issue is still pending.

Official notification and recruitment procedures

The procedures for recruiting employees are covered in article 16 of the Workers' Statute and in article 24 of the basic employment law. Employers must notify their local office of the state employment service, INEM, of any vacancies. An employer will be given permission to recruit freely if:

- There is no convenient INEM office.
- INEM cannot provide suitable candidates within three days.
- Candidates sent by INEM are unsuitable.

In practice there is little to stop an employer contacting a candidate direct, completing the employment contract requirements and *then* notifying INEM of the vacancy.

INEM is supposed to vet and reject advertisements which may be discriminatory but in many cases approval is a virtual formality, and advertisements specifying gender, regional preference, preferred age or linguistic origin appear.

Royal decree 1/1986, article 7, also introduced a new form of direct recruitment by which companies may arrange public competitive selection, using objective tests, provided three days elapse between the notice of recruitment and the tests. Again, INEM must be notified beforehand as well as informed afterwards of any resulting job contracts.

Collective agreements often contain provisions which specify both application and selection procedures. In the chemical industry, for example, anyone who has already worked in the company on some form of temporary or part-time contract is given priority when full-time vacancies occur. Management may determine recruitment procedures, but workers' representatives, who monitor recruitment, will be fully informed. In engineering, managements must inform workers' representatives of any post to be filled and of the selection procedure to be followed. At Citroën existing employees or former employees' family are given priority when filling permanent posts, provided their qualifications and skills meet the requirements. Management must consult the workers' representatives about the selection tests to be used, but has a free choice when selecting candidates for managerial or key posts.

State aid in the recruitment process. The state can give help to the unemployed who are prepared to take up a job offer in another part of the country. In such a case the Ministry of Labour provides a second-class rail ticket and a modest daily allowance. If the job is for more than twelve months the Ministry also pays removal expenses for the family, up to a maximum of Pta 135,000 (£735) and offers help with finding temporary accommodation, child care, medical care and relocation advice. There is a similar assistance programme for workers and their families who emigrate abroad.

Under EC directive 1984/636 there is help for young workers aged between 18 and 30 to take part in work exchange programmes ranging from three weeks to eighteen months' duration. In such cases, financial help may be available to cover travel expenses, lodging and subsistence.

Atypical work

Fixed-term contracts are a relatively recent development in Spain. They became generally permissible only in 1981, but only for certain categories of 'disadvantaged' employees. Since 1984 legislation has gradually increased the range of permissible temporary contracts, seen as contributing towards job creation. Legislation prescribes the conditions applying to fixed-term contracts in detail. At present there are nine principal types of fixed-term contracts. A booklet is available in English from the Ministry of Labour and Social Security explaining the regime (*Programmes Supporting Job Creation and Types of Contract*).

Fixed-term contracts can be concluded:

- For launching a new activity (not more than three years nor less than six months from commencement of activity: may be renewed for periods of not less than six months but continued employment after three years will render the contract indefinite).
- For hiring an unemployed worker (not longer than three years or less than six months), but not to replace an unjustly dismissed worker, or redundancy or dismissal on technical grounds in the previous twelve months.
- For a definite purpose (with termination subject to an agreed period of notice.
- For an increased work load (a maximum of six months in a twelve-month period).
- To replace an absent worker whose post is reserved.

In the period January–November 1989 2,140,000 fixed-term contracts of various kinds were concluded, compared with 1,988,000 for the whole of 1988. The total number of new employment contracts during this period was 4,003,500. According to recent figures from Eurostat for 1989, fixed-term contracts account for 0 per cent of employment.

Part-time employment contracts were not permitted until 1981. In 1989, a total of 356,258 contracts were registered. Part-time employment is now a major and steadily growing part of the labour market, with some 1·6 per cent of men and 12·8 per cent of women of the total work force employed on part-time contracts.

Part-time contracts are permitted for employment up to two-thirds of 'normal working time', defined as hours per day, hours per week, days per week or days per month. Such contracts must be in writing, on the official model form, specifying the nature of the contract and agreed hours. Part-time employment contracts can be either for a fixed period or permanent, and must be registered with the employment office, INEM. A copy of the contract must also be submitted to the social security office, together with social security registration. Social security contributions are *pro rata* to the time actually worked.

Temporary work agencies have no legal standing, but companies may be authorized to provide 'contracted services'.

Finding the applicant

Agreed and statutory provisions

Equal opportunities. In general terms, issues relating to discrimination or invasion of privacy are covered by the 1978 constitution—particularly articles 14–29—and will be dealt with under civil law. The general constitutional safeguard of equality of opportunity and non-discrimination is repeated in the Workers' Statute of 1980, particularly in article 4. The Instituto de la Mujer, now part of the Ministry of Social Affairs, has conducted several investigations into the working conditions of women and has presented proposals for increasing opportunities which the government has adopted and structured in a formal plan, aimed at broadening the employment, health, educational and cultural opportunities of women in a wide range of ways.

Collective agreements lay down various provisions in the field of equal opportunities. The chemicals agreement establishes a separate committee to study the effects of discrimination on women in the chemical industry. The engineering agreement pledges equal opportunity in employment, training, promotion and career development. It also proposes that job descriptions, the organization of work and working conditions should be designed to offer equal access to men and women. At company level, Repsol has set up a joint committee whose aim is to analyse the situation and take steps to increase the presence of women in traditionally male jobs.

Privacy. The *Ley organica sobre el derecho al honor, a la intimidad y a la propia imagen* (1982) protects the individual from undue investigation or interference and has particular relevance with regard to invasion of privacy. In practice, however, there are no codes of practice or other legal limitations determining the conduct of recruiters.

Recruitment techniques

There are three main ways of finding a candidate, in the following order of importance:

- Through the offices of INEM.
- Through advertising in the media.
- Through 'indirect' recruiting, such as speculative applications or word of mouth.

INEM is useful in finding skilled manual workers, but specialist and managerial staff are recruited either by direct advertising or through search and selection firms.

Advertising in the media

As mentioned earlier, INEM is supposed to vet and, where necessary, reject advertisements which may be discriminatory. In practice, however, this is not always done and advertisements frequently stipulate the maximum age, the place of residence or completed (compulsory) military service as conditions.

Only a few newspapers carry job advertisements. The daily *El País* has a wide selection of jobs in all sectors and at all levels in its Sunday business supplement, while the business weekly *Actualidad Económica* carries adverts for managerial positions. It is customary, particularly with large companies and multinationals, to give a brief outline of the company's activities and work force in an advertisement.

A new fortnightly magazine, *Employ*, was launched in early spring 1990. It deals with labour market matters in general and carries vacancies and 'jobs sought' notices. The publishers, Employ S.A., have a databank, Dataemploy, which holds details of job applicants and vacancies. It operates as follows. Employ will accept C.V.s, which can be matched to vacancies. Candidates' details are initially sent anonymously to employers, and if the employer shows interest the work seeker will be given details of the employer and position. Full candidate details will be sent to the employer if the work seeker wants to pursue the vacancy. Employ is not involved in the actual selection process.

Employment agencies

Spanish legislation formally prohibits private employment agencies from recruiting workers, the task being theoretically reserved to the state system, INEM. However, the basic employment law allows employers to advertise for vacancies after INEM has vetted the advertisement so long as the job number allotted by INEM is shown on the advertisement.

On the same principle, 'personnel selection agencies' (*empresas de selección*) are allowed to advertise on behalf of clients looking for permanent staff provided the notice is approved by INEM and the appropriate INEM job number is cited in the advertisement.

The same provisions also allow executive selection and search companies to function, and recognized shortages of managers in Spain, accentuated by above-average growth in the late 1980s, has provided a basis for this area of recruitment to grow rapidly. According to the recent *Economist* study, there were about twenty-five search and twenty selection firms, carrying out some 1,000 searches a year.

The search market is largely unregulated, except for the dictates of business ethics and commercial common sense, and headhunters are allowed to keep databases of potential candidates. Typical cost would be 35 per cent of first-year salary for a search, and 10–15 per cent plus costs for selection.

Details of consultants can be found in a directory entitled *Thesauro de la consultoria empresarial y jurídica* published by Editora Profesional (see appendix).

Graduate recruitment

Most universities have an office of the INEM-affiliated COIE (Centro de Orientación e Información y Empleo), which has a twofold task: firstly, it provides general information and documentation concerning career guidance, further education and postgraduate courses available both in Spain and abroad. Secondly, COIE offices will help graduates to find their first job by providing information on the labour market at large and on vacancies in particular. COIE offices maintain job banks to which individual companies report existing vacancies, with emphasis on graduate training schemes. COIE offices do not recruit in the sense that they would handle the applications or arrange interviews but are merely an intermediary organization which benefits employer and prospective employee alike.

Actualidad Económica produces a guide in conjunction with the Spanish branch of AIESEC and Andersen Consulting which sets out details of recruiting firms, the careers on offer, and selection procedures. Details can be found in the appendix.

Application documents and selection

Candidates are usually requested to apply with a handwritten application, a C.V. and often copies of certificates, diplomas or proof of other relevant qualifications, as well as a recent photograph. A survey conducted in 1986 by the Centro de Investigaciones Sociológicos (Centre for Social Research, CIS) reports that, after a short initial interview, psychological or psychometric testing is usually the first serious step in the selection procedure of most companies, particularly medium-sized or large ones. Once a candidate has passed this preliminary selection phase, he or she will go through a series of interviews which will be of paramount importance in choosing the new member of staff. The number of interviews varies, but it is not uncommon to have as many as six. Depending on the level of responsibility, group discussions can also figure in the recruitment process.

How tests are used depends very much on the type of organization undertaking recruitment. Recruitment agencies and companies concentrating on selection, who traditionally advertise widely in the Sunday press, use many tests, partly to weed out manageable short lists from a large volume of applicants. These include IQ tests, as well as aptitude and psychometric tests. Testing is almost never undertaken by executive search companies, although graphological testing—after informing the candidate—is used by some search consultancies for senior appointments. Large firms may use tests, including personality tests for entry-level appointments, where the candidate lacks a track record of experience, but testing is not widespread in the corporate sector outside medium-sized or large organizations.

Employment incentives

Various grants are available for employers who create new jobs or employ certain types of employees. Such grants are available either at national level, through schemes managed by INEM, the Ministry of Labour, or at autonomous community or town-hall level. Below are listed the most important schemes, together with the prescribed procedure.

Incentives for employing sufferers from toxic syndrome. Companies which employ registered unemployed sufferers from *colza*, a toxic syndrome caused by adulterated cooking oil which affected a large number of Spaniards in the 1980s, on permanent contracts are entitled to a grant up to Pta 250,000 (£1,360) for a part-time contract and up to Pta 400,000 (£2,445) for a full-time contract. Employers are also exempt from paying social security contributions for the first twelve months in the case of full-time contracts or for eighteen months in the case of part-time contracts.

European Social Fund. A wide variety of grants are available for job creation, retraining, exchanges, and technical advice through the provincial offices of the Ministry of Labour. Applications must be made by 30 June of the year *preceding* the proposed activity. These grants are given for collaborative employment projects, co-financed with local or national bodies.

Increasing women's employment. Special employment contracts have been designed to boost the employment of women in professions or activities in which they are under-represented; this provides a grant of up to Pta 250,000 (£1,360) for employers who offer permanent contracts to unemployed women under 25, or to long-term unemployed women over the age of 25. The sum rises to Pta 500,000 (£2,720) if Social Fund money is available.

Local job creation schemes. Employers who undertake local collaborative projects initiating new schemes, and who accord priority to the unemployed aged under 25 or over 45, are eligible for financial and technical help. A wide variety of schemes are available. Fifty per cent of the technical assistance is reimbursed (or 100 per cent if the project is proposed by the authorities) and contributions towards pay amount to Pta 250,000 (£1,360) per employee for permanent contracts and twice that amount if there is Social Fund participation. The schemes also provide up to 50 per cent of the agents' fees. These grants are available from provincial offices of the Ministry of Labour.

Joint INEM and local authorities employment schemes. These schemes, agreed by contract, are between INEM and local authorities. In schemes involving direct labour, 75 per cent of employees must be registered unemployed, and in schemes contracted to companies, 50 per cent. Grants usually amount to between 40 per cent and 75 per cent of total labour costs and are administered by the provincial offices of INEM.

Other official aids to job creation include schemes whereby redundant employees may cash in all their unemployment entitlement to establish their own business or to join a worker co-operative. Similarly, there are official grant schemes for the unemployed going on vocational training courses.

Many regional job creation schemes are also promoted by the Autonomous Communities into which the provinces have been grouped since 1981. One such example is the programme agreed in the province of Aragón in June 1989. An agreement between trade unions, employers' associations and the regional government (*junta*) created a provincial social and economic council, a programme of financial assistance to small and medium-size businesses and a training and job creation scheme.

Tax benefits for expanding the work force. An employer who achieves a net increase in the work force by taking on a full-time employee on a permanent contract is entitled to a reduction of Pta 500,000 (£2,720) per 'new employee year' in corporation tax due the following year.

Making the offer

The contract of employment

The contract of employment may be verbal or in writing, but in certain cases it *must* be in writing. It can be freely entered into by an employer and a person aged 18 or over, or **someone aged**

16 to 18 who lives independently or who has parental permission. All fixed-term contracts, contracts concluded for undertaking a specific task, and training contracts must be in writing. Either party can ask for a contract to be put in writing. Unless stated otherwise, contracts are presumed to be permanent.

Executives are not covered by many of the statutory provisions relating to ordinary employees. Their contract may be written or verbal—but it must be in writing in the case of an employee promoted to an executive position. The contract is understood to be permanent unless specified otherwise. Working hours, holidays and leave are agreed individually.

Job grading

On appointing an employee the employer is obliged to assign him a job grade (*categoría profesional*) as defined in the appropriate agreement or labour ordinance. This grading is important, as a grade defines the duties expected of the employee, the salary level as well as possibly the pattern of working hours, holiday entitlement, probation period, level of social security contributions, expenses entitlement, etc. Articles 23 and 39 of the Workers' Statute reinforce the employee's rights in this respect by providing safeguards when being moved to another job grade without consent.

Article 39 of the Workers' Statute defines a grade as a band which groups employees of similar ability, qualifications and responsibilities. There are no statutory restrictions on the grade to which an employer may appoint a recruit, but collective agreements often establish very specific rules about the percentage of the work force to be composed of each grade, as regards both recruitment and promotion procedures. Article 16.4 of the Workers' Statute does permit 'cross-grading' but it may prove difficult to determine which salary band applies to the employee. Problems may also arise when an employer wishes to move an employee to another grade. Articles 39 and 41 of the Workers' Statute do allow this to happen, either unilaterally or by agreement. There is substantial case law on the issue and the employer is required to keep good faith with the understanding about grading implied by the contract. To meet these points, and to introduce greater flexibility, several company agreements as well as some sectoral ones are moving towards rationalizing and reducing the number of grades. However, it is not uncommon to find agreements stipulating that when employees are moved to a higher grade they may request *demotion* after a suitable trial period, with no sanctions for incapacity. This is a very complicated area of labour legislation, and although the statute generally gives the employer considerable freedom to transfer employees there may be substantial limitations in collective agreements or labour ordinances.

Work and residence permits

Foreign employees. Residence and employment of foreigners are strictly controlled under the transitional arrangements for Spain's membership of the EC which apply until 1993. At present a residence permit is required for periods of residence of more than three months. A work permit is needed for most paid employment as well as self-employment. The procedure for obtaining the necessary papers is bureaucratic, lengthy and time-consuming. Substantial documentation is required for all types of permits, usually involving a medical examination and checking criminal records. An initial request is made at the Spanish consulate, which will determine the kind of permit applicable. There is a charge for each permit issued.

Exemptions. Certain categories of employees, listed below, are exempt from the need for a work permit. However, they do need a certificate from the Instituto Español de Emigración to declare them exempt:

- The self-employed originating in Gibraltar.
- Technicians and scientists employed by the Spanish government.
- Directors and teachers from foreign cultural and teaching institutions whose work in Spain is strictly the development of cultural programmes.
- Civil servants or military personnel involved in joint programmes.
- Media correspondents.
- Personnel from international scientific missions.
- Church staff.
- Performing artists involved in occasional performances.

Various *types of permits* are issued:

- *Type A*. For temporary work lasting not longer than nine months, renewable after a further three months have lapsed. The holder must leave Spain within fifteen days of its expiry. The labour authorities may require proof that the employer has advertised the post in the press or may insist that a Spaniard holding adequate qualifications is given the job.
- *Type B*. Valid for twelve months, renewable thereafter. This type of permit is likely to be granted to applicants with Spanish family connections.
- *Type C*. Valid up to five years; more likely to be granted to those with at least five accumulated years of residence and employment on other types of permits.
- *Type D*. For the self-employed, valid for up to twelve months. Preference may be given to those with Spanish family connections.
- *Type E*. For up to five years, for the self-employed whose Type D permit has expired.
- *Type F*. For up to three years, for certain categories of foreign workers living near the Spanish border.

Special permit for work experience. Valid for up to twelve months. Granted to those who wish to take employment on a 'work experience contract'.

Permit for EC citizens. This is a special permit applicable to *some* types of EC citizens, namely those who were permanently employed in Spain on 1 January 1986 (the date of EC accession), or for EC citizens who have since that date been granted a work contract for more than twelve months. In both cases the families of these EC citizens are also eligible for the permit. Certain groups of frontier residents, or the families of self-employed foreigners with certain residential qualifications, are also eligible. The permit usually lasts five years, although initially it may be granted for only twelve months.

Appendix

Organizations

Ministry of Labour and Social
Security (Ministerio de Trabajo
y Seguridad Social):
Agustín de Bethencourt 4
28003 Madrid
tel. +34 1 253 6000/253 7600
fax +34 1 233 2996

INEM (Instituto Nacional de
Empleo):
Calle Condesa de Venadito 9
28027 Madrid
tel. +34 1 585 9888
fax +34 1 268 3981/268 3982

Asociación Española de
Directores de Personal
(AEDIPE) (the Spanish
Association of Personnel
Directors):
Moreto 10
28010 Madrid
tel. +34 1 468 2217

Confederación Española de
Organizaciones Empresariales
(CEOE) (the Spanish
employers' organization):
Diego de León 50
28006 Madrid
tel. +34 1 563 9641
fax +34 1 262 8023

Instituto de la Mujer (equal
opportunity agency):
Almagro 36
28004 Madrid
tel. +34 1 410 5112

British Chamber of Commerce
in Spain:
Paseo de Gracia 11A
08007 Barcelona
tel. +34 3 317 3220
fax +34 3 302 4896
and in
Pl. Santa Barbara 10–1
28004 Madrid
tel. +34 1 410 7064
fax +34 1 410 4605

Publications

El País:
Miguel Yuste 40
28037 Madrid
tel. +34 1 754 3800
fax +34 1 204 8124

Employ SA:
Amado Nervo 2, Bajo C
28007 Madrid
el. +34 1 551 8300

Actualidad Económica:
Recoletos 1
28001 Madrid
tel. +34 1 431 0917
fax +34 1 276 8150

*Guía de las empresas que
ofrecen empleo* (graduate
recruitment guide):
contact *Actualidad Económica*

Editora Profesional (publishers of guide to management consultants in Spain):
Plaza Letamendi 37
08007 Barcelona
tel. +34 3 254 53 37

Further Reading and Information

European organizations

AIESEC (Association Internationale des Etudiants en Sciences Economiques et Commerciales) organizes recruitment events and placement both through its national organizations and at university level. The European headquarters is at:
40 rue Washington
1050 Brussels

FEACO (Fédération Européene des Associations de Conseils en Organisation):
Secretariat: 3 rue Léon Bonnat
75016 Paris
tel. +33 1 45 24 43 53
fax +33 1 42 88 26 84

CIETT
(Organization for employment agencies)
36–38 Mortimer Street
London W1N 7RB
tel. 071-323 4300

Selected reading and references

On employment law and practice

INCOMES DATA SERVICES monthly *European Report* monitors developments in employment law, pay, collective bargaining, and labour markets both at national and EC level.

INCOMES DATA SERVICES, *International Documents*, updated annually, provide detailed country-by-country information on commencement and termination of contract, and pay and conditions.

On labour markets

The figures quoted in the individual chapters were taken from:
ORGANISATION FOR ECONOMIC COOPERATION AND DEVELOPMENT (OECD), *Employment Outlook*, various years.

(continued)

ORGANISATION FOR ECONOMIC COOPERATION AND DEVELOPMENT, *OECD Economic Surveys*, published regularly on individual countries.
EUROSTAT (STATISTICAL OFFICE OF THE EUROPEAN COMMUNITIES), *Demographic Statistics 1988*.
EUROSTAT, *Labour Force Survey: Results 1987*.
EUROSTAT, *Employment and Unemployment, 1989*.
EUROSTAT and OECD publications can be obtained through Her Majesty's Stationery Office (Tel. 071-873 0011). The HMSO Bookshop is at 49 High Holborn, London WC1V 7HB.
German and other European projections have been published in:
PROGNOS AG/BUNDESANSTALT FÜR ARBEIT, *Arbeitslandschaft bis 2010*, (Nuremberg, 1989).
PROGNOS AG/BUNDESANSTALT FÜR ARBEIT, *Die Arbeitsmärkte im EG-Binnenmarkt bis zum Jahr 2000*, (Nuremberg, 1990).
WOLFGANG KLAUDER, 'Auswirkungen der politischen und wirtsfchaftlichen Entwicklung seit 1989 auf die Arbeitsmarktperspectiven', in *Mitteilungen aus der Arbeitsmarkt- und Berufsforschung*, 1/1990.
A basic digest of labour market statistics has been published by the INSTITUTE OF MANPOWER STUDIES entitled *The European Labour Market Review: the Key Indicators* (IMS Report No. 193, September 1990).

On graduate and general recruitment

ATS QUEST, *European Graduate Recruitment News*, provides regular coverage of graduate recruitment issues. (Available from ATS Quest, 0737-770013).
EUROPEAN COMMISSION, *Higher Education in the European Community*, fifth edition (Brussels-Luxembourg, 1988). English edition by Kogan Page.
A. J. RABAN, *Working in the European Communities* (Hobsons Publishing, London 1988) details education systems and graduate recruitment practices.
J. COURTIS, *Recruiting for Profit* (IPM, London, 1989).

On executive search

ECONOMIST PUBLICATIONS, *Executive Search and the European Recruitment Market* (London, 1990) sets out criteria for selecting a headhunter and examines individual firms in the UK and main European markets.

On advertising media

REED INFORMATION SERVICES, *Willings Press Guide*; an annual publication listing newspaper and specialist journals in the EC.